Structuralist Interpretations of Biblical Myth

Structuralist Interpretations of Biblical Myth

EDMUND LEACH

Professor Emeritus of Social Anthropology,
University of Cambridge

and

D. ALAN AYCOCK

Associate Professor, Department of Social Anthropology,
University of Lethbridge, Alberta

CAMBRIDGE UNIVERSITY PRESS

Cambridge
London   New York   New Rochelle
Melbourne   Sydney

ROYAL ANTHROPOLOGICAL INSTITUTE OF
GREAT BRITAIN AND IRELAND

Published by the Press Syndicate of the University of Cambridge
The Pitt Building, Trumpington Street, Cambridge CB2 1RP
32 East 57th Street, New York, NY 10022, USA
296 Beaconsfield Parade, Middle Park, Melbourne 3206, Australia

First published 1983

Printed in Great Britain at
The University Press, Cambridge

Library of Congress catalogue card number: 82-25263

British Library Cataloguing in Publication Data

Leach, Edmund
Structuralist interpretations of Biblical myth.
1. Man (Christian theology)
I. Title   II. Aycock, D. Alan

ISBN 0 521 25491 4
ISBN 0 521 27492 3 Pbk

CE

Contents

v

Acknowledgments

The publishers would like to thank the following institutions for permission to reproduce the plates. For those between pp. 66 and 67: 1, Vatican Library; 2, Yale University Art Gallery, Dura-Europos Collection; 3, State Hermitage Museum, Leningrad, U.S.S.R.; 4, National Gallery of Art, Washington D.C.; 5 and 6, Phaidon Press Ltd. For those between pp. 88 and 89: 1, 5, 6 and 7, Anderson-Alinari Archive, Florence; 2, 3, 8 and 9, Courtauld Institute of Art, London.

Royalties from the sale of this book have been donated by the authors to the Royal Anthropological Institute.

Plates

1 Introduction

EDMUND LEACH

None of the essays in this volume could have been written if they had not been preceded by Lévi-Strauss' two seminal essays, 'The Structural Study of Myth'[1] and 'The Story of Asdiwal,[2] but the discrepancies between the methodology developed here and that employed by Lévi-Strauss are numerous and fundamental.

Most of these differences stem from the fact that Lévi-Strauss follows the conventions of American cultural anthropology in supposing that human culture can be broken up into discrete entities. In his language, 'cultures', especially those of primitive peoples, exist in the plural. In almost all his myth analyses other than the 'The Story of Asdiwal' he is concerned with problems of cross-cultural comparison. In Lévi-Strauss' view, structuralist method provides illumination because it is able to reveal the existence of common patterned structures in the cultural products of contrasted 'cultures'.

As an indirect consequence of this emphasis on the plurality of cultures, Lévi-Strauss has been led to argue that his method can only appropriately be applied to data from what he calls 'cold' societies (i.e. 'primitive' pre-literate social systems) and not to data from 'hot' societies (i.e. literate, historically fluid social systems) in which the notion of cultural boundaries becomes wholly arbitrary.

As a functionalist British social anthropologist I reject this way of handling anthropological materials. For me, 'culture' is a concept which exists only in the singular. The permutations and transformations of patterned structure which I find interesting are not those which appear when we compare radically different social systems but those which are found within a single social system, both synchronically at one particular phase of its history and diachronically during the course of its historical development.

I emphasise this point right at the start because some commentators on my earlier, related essays[3] seem to have supposed that I fail to follow the precepts of Lévi-Straussian orthodoxy only because I fail to understand the essentials of the method. This is not the case. The essays in this book

1

employ variations of a structuralist methodology; it is a methodology which owes much to Lévi-Strauss; it is not a Lévi-Straussian methodology.

My first contribution to the general field covered by the essays in this book was published as long ago as 1961.[4] At that time Lévi-Strauss' *Mythologiques*[5] was not yet in existence and his earlier, mostly very brief, experiments in the structural analysis of myth were little known outside France.

Since then 'structuralism', 'post-structuralism' and the rest have gone through several cycles of death and rebirth in a variety of different fields – anthropology, literary studies, classical studies and biblical studies in particular. The term 'structuralism' itself, which arouses the awed admiration of some and the uncomprehending abuse of many, has by now acquired such a diffuse set of significations as to be almost meaningless. Was the psychoanalyst Lacan a structuralist? Are Althusser and Foucault to be reckoned structuralists? Was the structuralism of Roland Barthes derived from the structuralism of Lévi-Strauss or are they quite independent phenomena? Where does the Nietzschean 'Deconstruction' of Jacques Derrida fit in? Creeds and heresies and doctrinal deviations abound on all sides. It is hardly surprising that those who have not been caught up in this sectarian debate are inclined to brush the whole business aside as an ephemeral Parisian aberration.

That I think would be a pity. The basic argument that lies at the back of all the essays in this collection is that sacred texts contain a religious message which is other than that which can be immediately inferred from the manifest sense of the narrative. Religious texts contain a mystery; the mystery is somehow encoded in the text; it is decodable.

The code, as in all forms of communication, depends upon the permutation of patterned structures. The method of decoding is to show what persists throughout in a sequence of transformations.

When structuralist method is described in language of this sort it can sound very alarming but the principles involved are quite familiar, especially in theological studies. Christian dogma presupposes that the stories of the Old Testament 'prefigure' those of the New and that the deepest mysteries of Christianity are revealed in contemplation of the 'messages' in the text which survive this process of transformation.

Prior to the Reformation all Christians took this for granted. Not only was the whole of the Bible true but it was all true in the same way. It could be read as a synchronous story in which the different parts were internally cross-referenced.

It is only during the last 150 years that a quite different attitude has come to dominate biblical scholarship. Truth is now equated with 'historical truth' and since it has become apparent that large parts of the Bible

2

could not possibly be 'true as history' in a strict sense the task of the scholar has been seen as that of sifting the true from the false. If only we could know what really happened in history then we should understand the truth, including religious truth.

This type of biblical scholarship, which I have referred to as 'unscrambling the omelette', is not universal but it is very common. It seems to me to be a self-defeating exercise. Not only is the search for historical truth vain in itself, but the method of search serves to generate a fog which hides the religious truth that was formerly understood.

A methodology in which the Bible is treated piecemeal as a composite set of documents of varied date and differing authenticity is common to all the forms of scholarship which have their roots in the Higher Criticism of the nineteenth Century. By its very nature it serves to obscure, or even to deny, the existence of 'patterns' which persist as transformational structures between one document and another.

Structuralist analyses of the sort presented here reverse this procedure. They seek to make explicit coded patterns of the sort that the early Christian Fathers took for granted but which many latter-day Bible-readers seem to be unable to recognise.

Many not all. There will certainly be some readers of these essays who will react by saying: 'But of course, we know that, but it is trivial.' To such readers I have nothing further to say. But I think that there may be others who will react in a different way: 'But yes, I had not noticed that; it certainly seems curious; perhaps it is significant; let me think about it.' It is to open-minded Bible-readers of this latter sort that this book is primarily addressed.

It is also addressed to professional anthropological colleagues, but what they may or may not get out of it I cannot predict.

The circumstances through which these essays have all come to be published between one set of covers and under the sponsorship of the Royal Anthropological Institute need to be explained. The central point is that the RAI has a kind of moral obligation to publish Chapter 3 which was the Huxley Lecture for 1980 but which is substantially longer than most of the papers which appear in the RAI journal, *Man*.

The joint authors have never met. Dr Aycock's contributions are here because he sent me an earlier draft of 'The fate of Lot's wife' (Chapter 6), which might perhaps have been called 'Asdiwal in Jericho', at about the time that I had started to work on 'Why did Moses have a sister?' (Chapter 3), and I thought that the two pieces together might well go into an RAI Occasional Paper. Our book, as now published, is a much more ambitious exercise, but I would recommend any reader who is puzzled as to just what we mean by structuralist analysis to get the feel of things by reading Chapter 6 first; it is very short.

On such a first encounter the method is unlikely to appear either particularly illuminating or altogether persuasive, but Aycock here invokes many of the pattern-searching devices which appear in the longer essays: the assumption that all symbols are 'polysemic' – they have several different levels of meaning; the assumption that the structured patterns which convey other than superficial meaning are built up from contraries in binary pairs; the crucial value attached to the ambiguous 'middle term', in this case Lot's Wife herself; and so on.

In the Asdiwal story on which Aycock had modelled his interpretation, Asdiwal, who has one home under the sea and another in the sky and still another in the land of mortals, loses his magic powers and ends up turned to stone, betwixt and between, half-way up a mountain side. Because of this Asdiwal connection, the argument in this Aycock essay will appear more straightforward to the anthropologist reader than to the non-anthropologist. But if, when tackling the longer pieces, the reader keeps in mind the list of ambiguities on which Aycock lays stress in the last few paragraphs of his essay, it will become apparent that the two authors have independently made use of a very similar set of parametric variables.

I am rather less happy about Dr Aycock's second essay (Chapter 7), not so much because I disagree with it as because I think he has left out too much. An elaboration of that comment may help the non-anthropologist to understand just what we are up to.

The transformational scheme of binary oppositions which Aycock displays could be summarised as in Figure 1. But in claiming that, if we add in the details which Aycock mentions, Jesus and Cain are revealed as hero-figures which are 'precise structural analogues of one another' Aycock leaves out a crucial step in the argument. The stories of Jesus and of Cain may be analogues but, at least at the first level of transformation, they are inverse.

Cain founds a city of mortal men; Jesus founds a Church of immortal men. Sinful Cain becomes tied to God (is redeemed) through the sacrifice of Abel. Jesus is tied to God from the start; he redeems sinful mankind by submitting to sacrifice by the sinners who are redeemed.

In the patterning of these two stories Jesus is the equivalent of Abel rather than of Cain.

It may seem hardly polite to start off by criticising my colleague's contribution in this way. But I do so because my comment enlarges Aycock's thesis without destroying it. This is an important point. Structuralist analyses do not yield solutions which are 'right' or 'wrong'; they

4

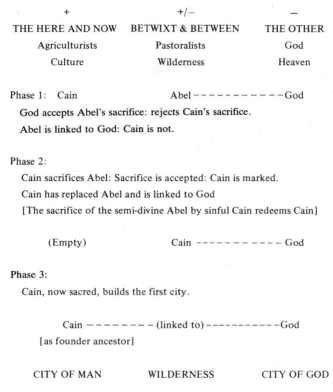

+	+/−	−
THE HERE AND NOW	BETWIXT & BETWEEN	THE OTHER
Agriculturists	Pastoralists	God
Culture	Wilderness	Heaven

Phase 1:   Cain   Abel – – – – – – – – –God

    God accepts Abel's sacrifice: rejects Cain's sacrifice.

    Abel is linked to God: Cain is not.

Phase 2:

    Cain sacrifices Abel: Sacrifice is accepted: Cain is marked.

    Cain has replaced Abel and is linked to God

    [The sacrifice of the semi-divine Abel by sinful Cain redeems Cain]

       (Empty)   Cain – – – – – – – – – God

Phase 3:

    Cain, now sacred, builds the first city.

      Cain – – – – – – – (linked to) – – – – – – – – –God

    [as founder ancestor]

    CITY OF MAN   WILDERNESS   CITY OF GOD

Figure 1. The structure of the Cain and Abel story.

demonstrate the existence of partial patterns. This provokes us to ask: is this significant or is it trivial? Further analysis will then reveal a more elaborate or perhaps a rather different pattern and we are faced with the same question as before: does this give us 'insight' or does it not?

There is no end point at which the analyst can say: 'there, I understand it all'. At best he can simply feel that he understands rather more than when he started out. The whole process is dialectical; a provisional enquiry which then provokes further enquiry. What is revealed is not the truth but the basis for looking at familiar materials in a new way.

Of an earlier paper of mine the distinguished Judaic scholar Jacob Neusner wrote: 'Leach will show us in stories we have read many times, meanings and dimensions we did not know were there. When we follow his analysis, we realize that we have been blind. For he shows us what it means to see.'[6] My hope is that some readers at least will feel the same way about the essays in the present collection, though I should add that the earlier part of Chapter 2, because of the circumstances of its original presentation, is not concerned with structuralist analysis at all.

Chapter 4 has also appeared before. The justification for reprinting it is that the 'Proceedings of the Royal Anthropological Institute', in which it originally appeared, only ran for a few years and is now extinct. Various would-be readers have complained that it is hard to obtain.

In the collection as a whole there is inevitably some instability of style and also a certain amount of repetition. My two RAI addresses (Chapters 4 and 3) and Dr Aycock's two papers presuppose an audience of anthropologists; Chapter 2 was prepared for a gathering of Bible scholars; Chapter 3 was a contribution to a joint seminar of literary critics and theologians; only in the last case did I prepare my text with an eye on the fact that the various pieces now assembled would all be printed in one place.

Despite this diversity of origin I have endeavoured throughout to keep the interests of the general reader in mind. We are not addressing ourselves to specialists though I hope that I have included enough scholarly apparatus in the footnotes to show my non-anthropological professional colleagues that I am not wholly ignorant of the fields in which they work.

Throughout the book quotations from the Bible are ordinarily given in the language, chapter and verse of the 1611 'King James Version'. I have however consulted a variety of other versions. In a few cases I make reference to translations employed in the New English Bible of 1970.

Notes

1 Lévi-Strauss, C. 1955 'The Structural Study of Myth' in *Journal of American Folklore*, Vol. 68. No. 270
2 Lévi-Strauss, C. 1958 'La Geste d'Asdiwal' in *Annuaire 1958–59* École pratique des hautes études. Section des sciences religieuses. Paris. pp. 3–43. Latest English version in C. Lévi-Strauss *Structural Anthropology: Volume II* (London: Allen Lane) pp. 146–197
3 Leach, Edmund 1969 *Genesis as Myth and Other Essays* (London: Cape)
4 Leach, Edmund 1961 'Lévi-Strauss in the Garden of Eden: an examination of some recent developments in the analysis of myth' *Transactions of the New York Academy of Sciences* Series 2. Vol. XXIII No. 4. pp. 386–96
5 Lévi-Strauss, C. 1964–71 *Mythologiques*: 4 Volumes. (Paris: Plon)
6 Neusner, J. 1979 *The Talmud as Anthropology*, Annual Samuel Friedland Lecture, The Jewish Theological Seminary of America

2 Anthropological approaches to the study of the Bible during the twentieth century*

EDMUND LEACH

> Old Testament stories were retained and rewritten because a small group of Jews ... believed themselves to be the sole survivors of the Hebrew people whose glorious traditions ran back into the dim past. They re-used the old stories, adapted them in up-to-date preaching to the needs of their own age ... There is a human reason why each story and saying was written and retained when so much was discarded and lost, and it is much more important in biblical study to try to discover why a story was told or a saying recorded than to question its date, origin or historicity.
>
> J. N. Schofield, *Introducing Old Testament Theology*
> (London: SCM Press Ltd [1964] pp. 9–10).

I had better say right away that my whole contribution will be an exercise in self-justification and that it will be very restricted in scope.

I am going to talk about anthropologists who have had the temerity to write about the Bible and *not,* to any significant extent, about biblical scholars who have, in one way or another, made use of the writings of anthropologists. Furthermore I am going to talk almost exclusively about British anthropologists rather than about American or French or Dutch anthropologists, or whatever. And finally I am going to take a very narrow view of what constitutes anthropology.

I am adopting this restricted position simply because there is too much ground to cover. I am fully aware that thereby I shall leave out much that some members of my audience may feel is both relevant and important. For example, I shall not be referring to the semiotic studies of biblical texts which have been inspired by Claude Chabrol and Louis Marin,[1] though in fact some of their work comes much closer to my own than does that of any of the British authors whom I shall mention. I shall also be ignoring the American counterpart of these French studies, most of which has appeared in the periodical *Semeia*.[2] My justification is simply

*Lecture given as a 'Centennial Address' to the meeting of the Society of Biblical Literature meeting in Dallas, Texas, 6 November 1980 (I am indebted to the organisers of the meeting for permission to reprint the text of the address. E.R.L.) It is printed in Tucker, G. M. and Douglas A. Knight (ed.) 1982 *Humanizing America's Iconic Book*, Chico, Calif., Scholars Press.

that the authors concerned are specialists in semiotics rather than anthropology.

Those who wish to explore some of the facets of my theme which I myself have neglected may find it useful to take a look at Rogerson (1978). Rogerson is not himself an anthropologist and his understanding of contemporary anthropological argument is, in places, decidedly mixed up. But he has read quite widely in parts of the relevant anthropological literature which I shall be ignoring in this lecture. Moreover, he makes a serious, if not wholly satisfactory, attempt to pin down the areas where anthropologists and biblical scholars get into a mutual tangle by using a similar terminology to denote quite different ideas.

I must confess however that I myself found Rogerson's book somewhat depressing, for whereas he ends by saying that 'some sort of new dialogue between Old-Testament experts and anthropologists is opening up,[3] his book makes it all too clear that, so far, there has been absolutely no mutual communication between the two sides. And here Rogerson himself is just as much at sea as are those of his theological colleagues whom he is seeking to inform.

My own professional competence is that of a social anthropologist trained in the British functionalist tradition established by Malinowski in the 1920s. As part of that tradition I use the word *myth* to mean 'a sacred tale about past events which is used to justify social action in the present'.[4] By this definition a myth is *true* for those who believe in it; whether it is also true in a matter-of-fact, empirical, sense is irrelevant and would, in any case, usually be very difficult to demonstrate.

Many people, including fellow anthropologists, use the word myth in quite a different sense. They assume that the essence of myth is that it is 'mythical', that is to say that it is *untrue* in any rational matter-of-fact sense. They therefore restrict the category to stories which contain palpably supernatural happenings: animals who talk, men who fly like birds, supernatural births and so on. Claude Lévi-Strauss, who has written more about myth than any other living anthropologist, appears to use the word in this way, though I am not aware that he has ever actually said so.

For my present purpose the distinction between the use of myth to mean 'a sacred tale' on the one hand and 'a fabulous impossible tale' on the other is very important. In the 'sacred tale' version, which is my own usage, the whole of the Bible is myth for Christians and the whole of the Old Testament is myth for Jews. In the 'fabulous impossible tale' version the scope of Biblical myth is not only much more restricted but also open to dispute. Even devout Christians would now

8

presumably agree that the Genesis Garden of Eden story is a myth in this latter, 'fabulous-impossible', sense, but there could be wide disagreement, even among the faithful, as to how to classify the New-Testament stories of Christ's Nativity.

When I declare that 'the whole of the Bible is myth' *in the sacred tale sense* I am merely stating the obvious, but I am also drawing attention to the nature of the canon. The Bible, as we have it today, is an edited compendium of a great variety of documents of differing origin and differing date. The sacredness of the corpus derives from the fact that it is these documents and these documents alone that the faithful are required to accept. In the process of editorial selection many other similar documents, some of which are known to us, were rejected. In other words, the canon is what it is because the final editors of the period 200 B.C. to A.D. 200 felt that these particular documents hang together in some special way.

This hanging together is crucial. It is what the books of the Old Testament say as a collectivity which makes it a sacred tale for the Orthodox Jew; it is what both the Old and the New Testament say when taken together as a single collectivity which makes the whole Bible a sacred tale for the believing Christian.

Now what these two canons say as collectivities is something very different from what the individual documents contained in the two canons say if they are read piecemeal. As an anthropologist concerned with myth in the 'sacred tale' sense, my interest is with the totalities rather than with the component parts of which the totalities are made up. Since a great deal of traditional-style biblical scholarship has precisely the opposite objective of taking the present-day collectivity apart in order to demonstrate what were its original component elements, communication between anthropologists of my sort and biblical scholars proper is often very difficult.

The difficulties are of many different kinds but one of them relates to the problems of how we should distinguish between *myth*, in the sense that I have defined, and *history*.

A countless number of events have occurred in the historical past. It should be obvious that even in the most favourable circumstances we can only know a tiny fraction of such past events. It should also be obvious that, for the most part, what we thus know is a matter of fortuitous accident rather than human planning. But though we may not know much about the past we can invent a great deal.

Down to about 1930 most anthropologists considered that this was their main task; they were pre-historians. Their role was to concoct plausible guesses about how grand-scale history had worked itself out.

9

Some anthropologists still operate within this convention. I myself do not. It seems to me that it is just as difficult to reconstruct the past as it is to predict the future.

Furthermore, since I totally reject all those forms of historicism which assume that the future must necessarily follow the same kind of trajectory that has been patterned by the past, I regard the invention of conjectural history as a total waste of time. The latter part of this personal credo has only an indirect bearing upon what I am going to say but you need to keep it in mind.

Now if we consider the Bible as a totality, as I urge you to do, it is quite clearly a sacred tale and not a history book. But, if you take the totality to pieces after the fashion of orthodox biblical scholarship, it is equally clear that substantial parts of it are written 'as if' they were history, and the majority of biblical scholars seem to have persuaded themselves that these are, in fact, records of 'true' history.

There is disagreement about just where legend ends and history begins but mostly it seems to be assumed that Moses (probably), and Saul and David (certainly), were real people who actually existed in the period 1250 to 1000 B.C., that is to say 500 years before the age of Herodotus and Thucydides.[5]

Personally I find this most implausible. There is no archaeological evidence for the existence of these heroes or for the occurrence of any of the events with which they are associated. If it were not for the sacredness of these stories their historicity would certainly be rejected. Classical scholars do not now believe that the Trojan War was an historical event or that the kind of society depicted in the Iliad and the Odyssey ever actually existed; still less do they imagine that Achilles and Hector and Agamemnon and the rest were real people of flesh and blood. But Saul and David were reputedly their contemporaries.

In this regard my own position is one of extreme scepticism. If we ignore the rather small number of named biblical characters whose existence is fully vouched for by independent evidence, and by that I mean archaeology rather than Josephus, I regard all the personalities of biblical narrative, both in the Old Testament and in the New, as wholly fictional. They are there because they fill a particular role in the totality of the sacred tale and not because they actually existed in history. And even if a few of them did have some kind of real-life existence this fact is quite irrelevant.

If a named individual 'X' 'really existed' so also did thousands of other individuals whose names we do not know. What interests us about 'X' is the role he is made to play in the sacred tale; this interest is not affected by the question of historicity. In Tolstoy's novel *War and Peace* quite a

10

number of the characters in the early part of the book are genuine historical personages who played a part in the war of 1812 between the Russians and the French, but the bearing of this fact on the significance of the novel is negligible. The marginal historicity of some features of the Bible story seems to me to be exactly comparable.

But this distinction between myth and history has another aspect. The view that I adopt – that the biblical narrative is a myth, a sacred tale – implies that I treat the entire text as synchronic. In the story one thing happens after another, because that is the only way you can tell a story. But the truth of myth, which is religious truth, is all of a piece. As in a dream, the end is already implicit in the beginning; there is no development, only dialectical inversion. Christ is the second Adam; the Virgin is the second Eve; sinless immortality replaces sinful mortality; and so on.

But if you adopt an historian's stance then you must look for diachronic development. The details which come later in the story refer to events which happened later in real time. And what comes later is not just a transformation of what came earlier but a complete replacement, an innovation.

A recent anthropological advocate for this approach to biblical materials, as against my own, is Professor Julian Pitt-Rivers.[6]

Pitt-Rivers is not prepared to defend the strict historicity of the Bible in an unqualified way. He does not, for example, claim that Jacob was an historical personality who lived to be 130 years old. But he does argue that because the Genesis story about Dinah comes in Chapter 34, while the Genesis story about Abraham lending his sister-wife Sarah to Pharaoh comes in Chapter 12, therefore, in real history, the morality of the Dinah story, which Pitt-Rivers sees as entailing the principle of Honour that still operates throughout the Mediterranean area, superseded the morality of the wife-lending story, which also has modern analogies but only in what Pitt-Rivers seems to regard as relatively primitive contexts.

Comparably he holds that the story of the Levite and his concubine in Judges 19, which is closely modelled on the story of 'Lot and the Angels of Sodom' in Genesis 19, represents a progression from the mode of myth to the mode of historical realism. He is prepared to rate the Lot story as myth because it includes palpably supernatural events, but he holds that the Judges story, being cast in 'realistic' form, should be treated as a representation of real-life political events.

I find this a most extraordinary view. The Judges story is part of a longer sequence which includes Chapters 20 and 21 just as the Lot in Sodom story is a part of a longer sequence which includes the story of

11

Lot's wife and the incest of drunken Lot with his daughters. Structurally, the sequences in Genesis and in Judges are permutations of one another, but both are equally remote from 'real history'.

I shall presently return to this theme in order to explain my debate with Pitt-Rivers in greater detail, but meanwhile I must fulfil my obligation to give an account of the interactions between anthropologists and biblical scholars during the whole of the twentieth Century.

The anthropological study of the Bible did not begin in the year 1900 but, as it happens, that is quite a good point at which to start an account of it.

During the eighteenth and nineteenth Centuries most of the proto-anthropologists of the period left the Bible alone. The story of the Flood, which made Noah the ancestor of all Mankind, and the calculations of Bishop Usher (not to mention those of Sir Isaac Newton), which put the Creation of the World only a few thousand years behind the present, could not be easily fitted to the historical fact that the Americas were already inhabited before the arrival of Columbus.

But in any case, prior to the latter part of the eighteenth Century, hardly anyone had thought of the Bible as a text which might need to take account of materials external to itself. The Bible was the directly revealed Word of God; it could be used to throw light on what we know from other sources but it could not in turn be illuminated by those sources. To suggest otherwise was a dangerous heresy, as Galileo and others discovered to their cost.

Over the centuries the word Religion had gradually come to embrace other cosmological systems besides that of Judaeo-Christianity. The Greeks and the Romans and the Moslems and the Hindus and even the illiterate heathen of Africa and the South Seas were all allowed to have 'religions' of a sort, but comparative studies which discussed the relations between such systems nearly always managed to leave the Bible out of account.

From time to time Christian missionaries had claimed to encounter versions of familiar Bible stories among distant tribes of naked savages and this had produced a variety of extraordinary accounts of the wanderings of the Lost Tribes of Israel, but systematic attempts to discover the real history of biblical texts only developed in the latter part of the nineteenth Century and the anthropologists only became involved in the game right at the end of it.

As far as Britain is concerned this development is traceable to a quite specific historical event. In 1881 the erudite polymath William Robertson Smith was dismissed for heresy from his Professorial Chair of Hebrew and Old Testament at Aberdeen.[7] He was then almost immediately appointed Editor of the *Encyclopaedia Britannica,* and within a few years was established as Professor of Arabic at Cambridge. He there developed a close friendship with a fellow Scotsman, a young classical scholar named J. G. Frazer. Smith had already endeavoured to show that the general anthropological theory of the day had relevance for an understanding of Arabic culture and further that the details of Arabic culture had relevance for our understanding of biblical texts. But he now commissioned Frazer to write a number of anthropological articles for the encyclopaedia and then went on to persuade Frazer to direct the major part of his academic effort to anthropology rather than to study of the classics. It was Frazer, as author of *The Golden Bough,* who first made anthropology a fully respectable academic pursuit.

In this regard Frazer's present renown is largely undeserved. Most of what he himself contributed to the study of anthropology and comparative religion has proved worthless. On the other hand almost everything which anthropologists continue to value in the whole vast corpus of Frazer's writings was a direct derivation from the work of his mentor Robertson Smith.

I will not go into details, for it all happened a long time ago; but I shall skim over the story.

Prior to the 1930s the anthropological discussion of Christianity, considered as a religion comparable to other religions, remained very much hedged about either by reticence or by hostility. Smith and Frazer were among the reticent.

Thus, although Smith remained a committed Christian, the first edition of *Lectures on the Religion of the Semites* treated the theme of the slain God of Christianity as comparable to that of earlier Middle Eastern religious systems, but the second edition, completed just before Smith's death in 1894, omits this offending passage.[8]

Similarly much of the celebrity of Frazer's *The Golden Bough* had originally derived from the notoriety which attached to what he had said in the second edition, that of 1900, about the Crucifixion of Christ as an example of a dying-god sacrifice. But in the third edition this section is relegated to a hard-to-find Appendix,[9] while in the well known, one-volume, abridged, edition of 1922 it is cut out altogether.

In a very similar way the renowned British folklorist E. S. Hartland had made stories about supernatural birth one of the central themes not only of his three-volume *The Legend of Perseus* (1894–6) but also of the two-volume *Primitive Paternity* (1909); but the numerous stories of this genre which appear in the Bible receive scarcely any attention in either publication.

13

On the other hand there was, at this same period, another class of scholar (of whom J. M. Robertson was a notable example) who rewrote the works of Smith and Frazer with the quite explicit intention of exhibiting parallels between biblical Christianity and heathen religions. Their express purpose was to display Judaeo-Christianity as a form of archaic superstition.

Even by the 1920s there was scarcely any *positive* interaction between biblical scholars and anthropologists. Frazer's massive three-volume *Folklore in the Old Testament* was published in 1918 but it retained the convention of reticence. Frazer here explored the folktales of the whole world to find parallels for details of content in the Old-Testament stories. But the details which he considered were not such as might be likely to arouse passionate debate among theologians, either Jewish or Christian.

Thus Part I, Chapter 4 is a 250-page monograph entitled 'The Great Flood'. Less than 20 pages are devoted to the Bible story, and these simply repeat the textual criticism which was generally accepted by orthodox biblical scholars of the day. The rest of the chapter is a compendium of flood stories from all over the world. They are presented as a long list of separate items with little attempt at generalisation. Frazer notes that these stories of a universal flood cannot represent the folk memory of an historical event since they are contradicted by geological evidence. But he offers no explanation as to why stories of this kind should be so widespread or why they should be concentrated in some parts of the map rather than in others.

Even today there is no general agreement among anthropologists about such matters, yet there are a number of specifically anthropological observations of a structuralist kind which might have a bearing on the Genesis story.

For example, it is a characteristic of Flood stories that the survivors become the ancestors of all mankind. These survivors are related to one another in a variety of ways. Sometimes, though rather rarely, as mother and child or as brother and sister; sometimes as two orphans brought together by chance; sometimes, as in the Bible, as husband and wife and their married offspring.

What is common to almost all the stories is that the survivors are ordinary human beings who have been born in an ordinary way; they are thus quite unlike the first parents in the first Creation, who belong, like Adam and Eve, to some kind of Other World Paradise and who have come into being in some spontaneous irregular fashion.

Although these mysterious original first parents engage in sex relations in some fashion and thereby have offspring, it is a union that is contaminated with the sin of abnormality. The function of Flood stories is to destroy this first Creation and its ambiguities and to start again. The end of the Flood marks the beginning of true time. The intermediate period between the First Creation and the Flood is a kind of betwixt and between, an Other Time which is fitted to an Other World inhabited by Other Creatures who are not altogether men. The offspring of the Garden-of-Eden first parents and the offspring of the Flood-Survivor first human ancestors are contrasted as abnormal versus normal, sinful versus legitimate.

In the case of Noah, the survivors are legitimately married husbands and wives, so their offspring are in no way contaminated by similarity to the strange creatures of Genesis 6 who were the product of sexual cohabitation between the sons of God and the daughters of men. But Frazer discusses Flood stories and First Creation stories in quite different chapters and fails to recognise that they are in any way connected.

This comment could be applied to the whole of Frazer's immense exercise. Most of the biblical details which he chooses to discuss seem trivial; yet if they were to be treated in a different anthropological style they could appear interesting.

Here is a case in point which is relevant to what I shall be saying later. Chapter 1 of Volume 3 is entitled 'Keepers of the Threshold'. It runs to eighteen pages. The biblical reference is minimal – though, such as it is, it is consistent with the proposition that an aura of sanctity of some special kind attached to the threshold of the Temple at Jerusalem.

Frazer makes that point and then rambles around the world giving instances of ritual practices which suggest that thresholds are frequently sacred-tabooed localities. But the best that he can manage by way of an explanation is to say that: 'all these various customs are intelligible if the threshold is believed to be haunted by spirits'. Perhaps so; but Frazer offers no suggestion as to why thresholds should be haunted by spirits! Yet here again we are concerned with the ambiguities of betwixt and between.

Even before 1910[10] the associates of Emile Durkheim had already developed a sophisticated theory which explains in a very convincing way just why intermediate places and intermediate social conditions are likely to be treated as sacred, and therefore subject to 'taboo'.

Fined down to its essentials the argument runs something like this. Uncertainty generates anxiety, so we avoid it if we can. The categories of language cut up the world into unambiguous blocks. The individual is either a man or a beast; either a child or an adult; either married or unmarried; either alive or dead. In relation to any building I am either inside or outside. But to move from one such clear cut state to its opposite entails passing through an ambiguous 'threshold', a state of uncertainty where roles are confused and even reversed. This marginal position is regularly hedged about by taboo.

This finding clearly has an important bearing on my general topic of the relevance of anthropology to biblical studies. For, after all, mediation between opposites is precisely what religious thinking is all about.

Thresholds, both physical and social, are a focus of taboo for the same reason that, in the Bible, inspired sacred persons, who converse face to face with God, or who, in themselves, have attributes which are partly those of mortal man and partly those of immortal God, almost always experience their inspiration in a 'betwixt and between' locality, described as 'in the wilderness', which is neither fully in This World nor in The Other.

Frazer understood none of this, but I have given it emphasis here because the sacredness which attaches to entities which are ambiguous or intermediate is a key theme which links together the otherwise disparate approaches to the interpretation of religious symbolism which are to be found in the work of such contemporary British social anthropologists as Mary Douglas, Victor Turner, D. F. Pocock, and myself.

After Frazer, the next initiative for an interaction between biblical scholarship and anthropology came from the biblical-scholar side. In 1933 there appeared two books with rather similar titles: E. O. James' *Christian Myth and Ritual* and a collection of essays edited by S. H. Hooke *Myth and Ritual: Essays on the Myth and Ritual of the Hebrews in Relation to the Culture Pattern of the Ancient East*. Further exercises of the same sort appeared in later years and the production as a whole came to be known as the work of 'the Myth and Ritual School'.

James was Professor of Philosophy and History of Religions at Leeds; Hooke was Professor of Old Testament Studies in the University of London. Both had had some training in academic anthropology and were influenced not only by Frazer but by an intellectually more distinguished contemporary, A. M. Hocart.

Hocart rejected the item by item style of ethnographic comparison favoured by Frazer and adopted a semi-functionalist form of argument which held that social institutions need to be considered as constituent wholes which correspond to a limited number of ideal types. Thus he maintained that the rituals surrounding Kingship and the annual celebration of the New Year always have the same specifiable set of component parts.

It was from Hocart rather than from Frazer that Hooke and his associates picked up the idea that Ancient Babylonia, Ancient Egypt, and the Kingdom States of the Old Testament all conformed to a single 'culture pattern'. Taking this notion as axiomatic they then proceeded on the assumption that gaps in the sociological records of the Old Testament can be filled in by interpolating bits and pieces from the surviving documentary and archaeological records of other Ancient Middle Eastern Societies.

The outcome of this exercise was conjectural history of a very far-fetched sort. But the theologians in Hooke's company had the further objective of showing that the Christianity of the first Century A.D. represented an evolved and ethically sophisticated version of this same ancient (hypothetical) pattern.

In matters of biblical exegesis the recent work of Julian Pitt-Rivers to which I referred earlier has much in common with this latter aspect of the work of the Myth and Ritual School. My own very different position is that there was no such ancient common pattern. The imaginary historical past from which early Christian society is supposed to have evolved through the processes of history is, for the most part, simply the mythical projection of their own past which was believed in by Jews and Christians alike in the era of Josephus.

Oddly enough the relationship between biblical texts and non-biblical materials which was assumed by the various Christian apologists of the Myth and Ritual School was often very similar to that which had been proposed by J. M. Robertson, a generation earlier, in his efforts to exhibit Christianity as a tissue of antique superstitions.

Despite Hocart's explicit repudiation of the Frazerian method of cultural comparison, the *content* of much of the argument presented by these various essayists was a fairly direct borrowing from what Frazer had written about divine Kingship and dying gods in the pages of *The Golden Bough*; but the *form* of the argument derived from an earlier generalisation by Robertson Smith concerning the intimate interdependence of myth and ritual.

Smith had maintained that the heart of religion is to be found in religious practice (ritual) rather than in the verbal formulae of belief (myth) which are supposed to be expressed through ritual. The ritual is fixed and obligatory; what is believed varies from one worshipper to another and is inaccessible to the outside observer except in so far as it is enshrined in a dogmatic creed. In Smith's words: 'it may be affirmed with confidence that in almost every case the myth was derived from the ritual and not the ritual from the myth'.[11] Years later a rather similar point was made by the anthropologist Malinowski who wrote of myth as a 'charter for social action'.[12] Broadly speaking it is a position with which I agree.

Hooke and his colleagues seem likewise to have accepted this general proposition, but they then went on to make the entirely unwarrantable

17

assumption that the interdependence of myth and ritual is so close that if you know the myth you can infer the ritual from which it was derived. They claimed to have demonstrated that throughout the Ancient Middle Eastern World there had once been a unified system of ritual practice that was centrally concerned with divine kingship, sun worship and the cycle of the agricultural calendar; all of which has a certain plausibility but is not based on any genuine evidence. Strictly speaking it rates no better than a guess.

A reassessment of the whole enterprise was published in 1958 in a further collection of essays entitled *Myth, Ritual and Kingship*. Hooke was again the editor, but this time the remaining contributors were philologists and historians rather than anthropologists or theologians. The general view, which was much influenced by the arguments of Henri Frankfort,[13] was thoroughly sceptical. The ancient states of the Middle East had been nothing like so similar as Frazer and Hocart had suggested. Kingship is not a single unified institution. Hence we cannot infer anything about Kingship in Israel and Judah from a consideration of Kingship in Egypt or Kingship in Babylonia, or wherever.

And here again I agree. History cannot be reconstructed on the basis of homology. The only way we can learn anything about what happened in the past is by gaining access to contemporary evidence, either from documentary records which were written at the same time as the events they purport to record or from the evidence of archaeology. Legends and oral traditions of various kinds can be very interesting but are not history.

In the case of biblical materials few scholars would now want to maintain that any of the documents other than some of the letters to St Paul are strictly contemporaneous with the events which they purport to record. Anyone who asserts that, even so, these documents do represent an approximation to historical fact, needs to demonstrate that they are in accord with what archaeology has to tell us. But in fact, despite a vast amount of research, archaeology tells us very little; furthermore, what little it does tell us is nearly always in radical disagreement with the biblical record.

I should perhaps add that, in the United States, the E. O. James–S. H. Hooke technique for the blending of anthropology and the history of religions was given a new lease of life by the arrival of Mircea Eliade in Chicago in 1956. Eliade's best book *The Myth of the Eternal Return*, which dates from 1949, ranges far beyond the geographical limits of the Ancient Middle East, but his assumptions about how cross-cultural comparison may be considered to throw light on biblical materials are markedly similar to those of the Myth and Ritual School.

The Eliade manner in the field of comparative religion does not really fall within my brief. The *Festschrift* in his honour which was published in 1969[14] included articles by twenty-nine contributors but none of them were anthropologists and only two of them wrote on biblical themes.

So let me now turn to the work of some anthropologists whose style of argument is of a more modern sort.

The first occasion on which a British social anthropologist applied his skills to an interpretation of a biblical text was in October 1954 when Isaac Schapera gave his Frazer Lecture entitled 'The Sin of Cain'. The focus of Schapera's attention was the detail of the Cain and Abel story by which, although Cain was driven out into the wilderness as a punishment for his act of fratricidal homicide, he was nevertheless thereafter marked by God as a protected person. The gist of Schapera's argument is that there are many biblical texts which support the view that homicide among the Ancient Hebrews was considered to be a private delict; that is to say responsibility for reprisal did not lie with the State but with the near kin of the deceased. Homicide created a situation of feud which was resolved on an 'eye for an eye, a tooth for a tooth' basis.

Now there are many still-existing societies in which the general custom of feud-vengeance of this kind still prevails but it is very common to find that the offences of patricide and fratricide provide 'exceptions to the rule'. A blood feud calls for vengeance by the kin of the deceased against the kin of the assassin; but, if the deceased and the assassin are immediate kin, feud-vengeance is impossible and the destiny of the assassin, either for glory or oblivion, then becomes the direct responsibility of God. So, in Schapera's view, Cain was the beneficiary of divine protection because he was a fratricide as well as a murderer.

Schapera's essay deserves your attention but I myself feel that he largely missed the point. Cain was not only a murderer and a protected wanderer, he was the creator of civilisation, the founding ancestor who built the first city (Genesis 4.17). In one sense the killing of his brother is a mythical prototype of 'murder' but it is also the prototype of 'sacrifice'. By killing Abel, Cain replaces him, while at the same time he makes himself sacred. But this is not an appropriate occasion for the elaboration of that theme. And in any case, as I shall indicate presently, I do not myself believe that biblical texts can ever be illuminated by direct comparisons with modern ethnographic evidence.

Before I go further perhaps I should consider an issue of principle. What *could* anthropologists be expected to contribute to the study of the Bible?

I am in difficulty here because the various fellow anthropologists whom I have mentioned as having certain points in common with myself would certainly not give the same sort of answer to that question which I might

19

give myself. But if I indicate some of the areas where we are in disagreement, my own views will become apparent.

One widely held assumption is that anthropologists can illuminate biblical texts by drawing attention to ethnographic phenomena which are superficially similar to matters reported in the Bible. This was the basis of Frazer's approach and of works such as Morgenstern (1966). Morgenstern in fact writes: 'The monuments of ancient Semitic cultures unearthed in excavations, the Bible and other ancient semitic writings, and the records of classical and mediaeval authors, are supplemented by the varied and informative accounts of observant travelers and ethnologists of modern times. Hence our knowledge of these varied sources is sufficient to permit far-reaching conclusions.'[15] My own view is that the observations of the 'travelers and ethnologists of modern times' cannot help us at all. My fellow anthropologists do not all share this negative attitude to cross-cultural comparison.

Pitt-Rivers has expert knowledge of the social values of the contemporary peoples of the Mediterranean area and he believes that there has been an historical continuity between the cultural system recorded in the Bible and that with which he is himself familiar. This is perfectly possible, but there seems no good reason to believe it.

Pitt-Rivers seems to be thinking of a timespan covering about 3000 years. We know for certain that vast political upheavals have occurred during that period but we cannot possibly know whether any features of general culture have persisted throughout. There can be no case for reading biblical texts as if they were a record of remote history which, by some happy accident, becomes more intelligible if referred to the present!

My complaint against Mary Douglas is similar. Her well known discussion of the Abominations in Leviticus 11,[16] in which she maintains that the prohibited animals are all in some way anomalous and that the system as a whole is designed to exhibit God's approval of order and completeness, was an adaptation of her theories concerning the classification of animals among the Lele, a Central African people whom she herself had studied.[17] In so far as it concerns Leviticus, Douglas' essay is of considerable interest, but when she tries to strengthen her argument by resort to ethnographic comparison she is led into writing nonsense.

For example, it is quite clear that all the books of the Old Testament are addressed to a population of urban agriculturalists. Their imagined ancestors, the Israelites of the Pentateuch who wander in the never-never land of the sacred wilderness, are pastoralists only as ideal types. Moreover, not only were the Israelites of real history agriculturalists rather than pastoralists, but, as archaeology clearly demonstrates they were, at all times, very much mixed up with their non-Israelite neighbours. So it is wholly inappropriate that Douglas should try to support her Leviticus arguments by reference to present-day practices among the Nuer, a pastoralist people of the Southern Sudan.[18] As for the following argument about the pig, it seems to me totally absurd:

> As the pig does not yield milk, hide nor wool, there is no other reason for keeping it except for its flesh. And if the Israelites did not keep pig they would not be familiar with its habits. I suggest that originally the sole reason for its being counted as unclean is its failure as a wild boar to get into the antelope class, and that it is on the same footing as the camel and the hyrax, exactly as stated in the book.[19]

If anthropologists are to be taken seriously by other kinds of biblical scholar they need to do better than that!

Literary and archaeological evidence shows that in fact the pig was very plentiful through the Middle East from early neolithic times onwards. Furthermore, extreme ritual attitudes, both positive and negative, towards both pigs and pig meat were common in most of the ancient urban civilisations of the region.[20, 21]

So let me try to give you my own answer to the question: what might anthropology be expected to contribute to biblical studies?

Well first of all I hold that anthropologists need to make a case for saying that no part of the Bible is a record of history as it actually happened. Then, on the positive side, they can show that the whole of the Bible has the characteristics of mytho-history of the sort which anthropologists regularly encounter when they engage in present-day field-research. The similarity is a matter of structure not of content. Finally they can show that if biblical texts are treated as mytho-history of this kind, then the techniques which modern anthropologists employ for the interpretation of myth can very properly be applied to biblical materials. If this is done then some parts of the text will appear in a new light, or at any rate in a light which has not been generally familiar to Bible readers during the past four centuries. This new-old way of looking at things is not necessarily better than currently more conventional ways of looking at things, but it deserves consideration.

These are large claims; I have only time to indicate how they might be substantiated.

First of all I must emphasise that I completely reject Lévi-Strauss' view that a radical distinction can be drawn between what he calls 'hot' and 'cold' societies.[22] 'Hot' societies are sophisticated social systems with a literary tradition whose members are fully aware that they are caught up in an historical process of change and development; 'cold' societies are the primitive societies of anthropological literature in which there is no literary tradition and no sense of historical progression.

In 'cold' societies, so it is said, everyone behaves as if social life as it is now had been like that since the beginning of time and will continue like that for ever more.

Lévi-Strauss considers that his own theories have only marginal application to the culture of 'hot' societies. In particular, he holds that since the Bible is the product of a 'hot' society, it is quite inappropriate to attempt to apply to the study of biblical materials any kind of modified version of his own procedures for the study of myth.

For many years I have adopted a precisely opposite stance. It is true that societies with a tradition of literacy differ in important ways from societies which lack such a tradition, but the differences are not, in my view, of the kind which Lévi-Strauss suggests. All peoples everywhere imagine that they know quite a lot about their own history. That 'history' may be stored in traditional sagas, which are memorised by a few experts, or it may be recorded in books, but, in any social system, there is always someone around who is eager to tell the visiting stranger just how it all began and how things came to be as they are now.

Now 'history' of this sort, which explains how things now are, may or may not be true as a record of *actual* history. But the general probability is that it is not true in any matter-of-fact sense. I can illustrate why this is so from my own experience.

When I was engaged on anthropological fieldwork in North Burma in 1940 I was given, in great detail, three entirely different accounts of an inter-village war which was supposed to have taken place only forty years previously. I also, as it happened, had access to a contemporary account of the same matter written by the British colonial adminstrator who was in charge of the area at the time.

This last version, dating from 1900, was quite incompatible with any of the three oral versions given to me in 1940, but since the administrator in question clearly did not understand what was going on, his factual statement was no better as history than were the others. What was at issue was a matter of political rivalry and rights over land. I got three different versions because, in 1940, there were three different factions each with its own version of how things had come to be as they were. Even now I do not know what really went on around 1900, but, in order to understand the rivalries of 1940, it was quite essential that I should take account of all the different versions of the 'history' of the 1900 period.

I would claim that, in a backhand sort of way, this case history has relevance for our understanding of the Bible. For example, it is now fairly generally agreed[23] that the earliest of our present Gospel texts could not

22

have been put together before the destruction of Jerusalem by the Romans in A.D. 70. If so, then, at the very earliest, the Gospels were written forty years after the events they are supposed to record. Orthodox biblical scholars have usually overcome this difficulty by making two assumptions. First, they assume that forty years is not a very long time so that an oral tradition could survive such a period without much distortion. Second, they assume that the discrepancies between the different Gospel stories are minor and are to be explained by the circumstances of this period of oral tradition. If we put the Gospel stories together we have, at the core, a record of events which really happened in an historical sense.

I don't know how many members of this distinguished audience still take that kind of view; my anthropological experience leads me to the contrary conclusion that, while it is perfectly possible for real history to be embedded in oral tradition, the balance of probabilities goes the other way. Taken by itself oral tradition provides no evidence at all for what really happened.

And if we cannot be sure that any particular part of the New Testament is true as history, how much less confident can we be about the Old! And yet most Old-Testament scholars continue to write as if substantial parts of our modern text were a record of events which actually happened. They assume not only that the authors concerned had a serious interest in recording history in this factual, archival sense, but that they had the technical resources to make such records.

But in the second millennium B.C. the past was not viewed as a sequential chronology. The archival records of the ancient civilisations consist of lists of various kinds, including lists of the names of kings. But when we encounter narratives they are 'mythical' sagas such as the Gilgamesh epic. And the written versions of such narratives, which are all we now have, can only have been intended for the eyes of fellow scribes and schoolboys since no one else could read.[24] Not only that, but the Old-Testament stories, which scholars now rate as history – the saga of Saul and David for example – are nearly all of the intimate, but self-contradictory, mytho-historical kind which anthropologists encounter in their present-day fieldwork; the North Burma stories to which I referred just now are a case in point.[25]

But if the Bible is not true as history, it still remains a sacred tale, and there remains the problem of interpretation. Here the crucial anthropological point is one which would presumably be accepted by all but the most fundamentalist theologians. There is a theological meaning (or perhaps several theological meanings) which is *other than* the manifest meaning of the narrative as such. The meaning of the narrative as such appears to be plain. How can we progress from this superficial sense to the other (postulated) subliminal sense?

At the heart of the method which I advocate, which is a direct borrowing from a principle which Lévi-Strauss has used in other contexts, is the insistence that the really significant elements in biblical narrative are the contradictions.

Orthodox biblical scholarship of the nineteenth-Century sort disposed of the inconsistencies in the text by a careful process of unscrambling the omelette. It was shown that the text, as we now have it, is an edited compendium of a variety of distinct 'original' documents. But the main purpose of this scholarly endeavour was directed towards the reconstruction of the original documents; relatively little attention was paid to the problem of why the final editorial compilers of the canon should have acted as they did, passing on to posterity composite texts which are full of palpable inconsistency and transformed repetitions.

Why is the Adam of Genesis 1 given dominion over the whole Earth, but the Adam of Genesis 3 condemned to a life of permanent toil and sweat? Why is Moses the adopted son of Pharaoh's daughter at the beginning of Exodus 2, a prince among princes, but the son-in-law of a shepherd priest in the backside of the desert by the end of it? Why do we have four contradictory Gospels when one would have been so much less confusing? And so on.

The anthropologist Victor Turner has not, so far as I know, made any specific reference in his writings to such biblical contradictions but what he has written about structure and anti-structure in his book *The Ritual Process*[26] provides the beginnings of an answer to my question.

Turner's arguments, which derive fairly directly from what Van Gennep wrote about rites of passage at the beginning of the century, depend upon the view that what is valued in religious and para-religious experience is a sense of *communitas*, a feeling of intense social togetherness in which all the barriers of hierarchy which prevail in the rational secular affairs of everyday life are temporarily abandoned or even directly reversed. This sense of *communitas* is associated with a state of liminality, of being betwixt and between, neither in this world nor in any other. It is a mystical state to which the rules of strict logic do not apply.

Now in ritual performance the symbolisation of such intermediate states is fairly straightforward; the actors do exactly the opposite of what they would do in normal secular life. Those who normally wear very grand clothing go around naked or in rags; those who normally wear common clothing dress up in splendour. Hierarchies are reversed; masters wait on their servants; children give orders to their elders. Taboos on food and sex are either enormously intensified or abandoned

24

altogether; transvestite behaviour is common ... anthropologists can provide thousands of examples of this kind of symbolic coding. The life-style of contemporary hippies, who, whatever their limitations, certainly put strong emphasis on the values of *communitas*, provide a good example of what I mean.

But while confusion and inversion is readily employed in ritual action, it becomes self-defeating if it is employed in narrative. If narrative mytho-history is to serve as a charter for present-day religious and para-religious behaviour it cannot be gibberish; it must appear to make sense.

And that is how mythologies are presented. They do not exist as single stories but as clusters of stories which are variations around a theme. Each individual story seems to make sense by itself, but, if we take all the stories together, and assert, as a matter of dogma, that they are all 'true' at the same time, then we arrive at a nonsense because, in detail, the collectivity of stories is self-contradictory.

Yet, according to the liminality, betwixt and between, *communitas* argument, it is precisely the self-contradictions which carry religious significance. The analyst therefore must find some way of discovering the sense behind the non-sense.

In a lecture such as this, which is designed as a large-scale survey, it is hardly possible to give a satisfactory illustration of what is involved because, as in all forms of structuralist analysis, demonstration calls for the close comparison of a number of different texts in considerable detail. But I can perhaps show you the general idea by making brief reference to several well-known and seemingly unedifying Old-Testament stories.

Since Pitt-Rivers used two of these stories in his purported demonstration that my methodology is wholly misplaced, it may be appropriate if I now show that in fact they fit much better with my thesis than with his.

As I indicated much earlier on, the crux of the issue between us is that Pitt-Rivers holds that a clear-cut distinction can be drawn between the mythical, supernatural style of narrative which characterises the early chapters of Genesis, in which chronology does not really matter, and the historical-realistic mode of later parts of the Bible, in which progression from earlier to later is an essential part of the message.

I myself cannot discern any such distinction. God converses face to face with Samuel just as he does with Abraham and Moses. The Acts of the Apostles, despite a superficially realistic form, is almost as full of supernatural events as the Book of Genesis. Angels come to the aid of Peter in prison (Acts 12.5–7) just as they come to the aid of Lot in

Sodom (Genesis 19.10–17). Moreover the transformation of the Lot in Sodom story into the Levite in Gibeah story (Judges 19.22–30), which Pitt-Rivers uses as the paradigm for his contrast between myth and realism, entirely fails to support his thesis. I will now try to demonstrate this.

As I have indicated, I hold that the whole of the Bible is mythical and that all the individual stories in the total corpus need to be read as if they were synchronous. So let us start at the end and work backwards.

In the New Testament, Bethlehem is the birthplace of Jesus Christ, the messiah who is born to be king but who is also born to die as a sacrifice for the remission of sins. Bethlehem is given this distinction because of the prophecy in Micah 5.2: 'But you, Bethlehem in Ephrathah, small as you are among Judah's clans, out of you shall come forth a governor for Israel.'

Micah's prophecy is also a retrospective observation concerning 'history'. The Ephrathites from Bethlehem included the lineage of Elimelech, the husband of Naomi and the father-in-law of the Moabitess Ruth from whom was descended David, son of Jesse. The Ruth reference, like the Micah reference, puts Bethlehem in Judah (Ruth 1.1–2; 4.18–22).

However the first reference to Bethlehem in the Old Testament is at Genesis 35.16–20 where it is declared to be 'but a little way' from the birthplace of Benjamin and the deathplace of Rachel, who died in childbirth. This is consistent with 1 Samuel 10.2 which declares that the tomb of Rachel is in the territory of Benjamin. The context of this latter statement is the summoning of Saul to the kingship.

So Bethlehem-Ephrathah seems to be a betwixt and between sort of place, between death and birth, between lowliness and kingship, between Saul and David, a threshold to the new life. But everything which happens there seems to be consistently associated with sinless virtue.

Just the opposite is the case with Gibeah which is the locality where the horrid events of Judges 19 take place. Gibeah provides us with a paradigm of sin; the men of Gibeah behave like the men of Sodom. Its position is unambiguous. It is in Benjamite territory and is the home of Saul (1 Samuel 10.20–26; 11.4). Where Bethlehem stands for *communitas*, Gibeah stands for factional strife.

It is thus appropriate that the Levite's concubine, who is destined to die on the threshold and be sacrificially dismembered into separate pieces in Gibeah, should originally have come from Bethlehem, where the story starts (Judges 19.1–5). Also it is appropriate that her death, which is the direct consequence of the sin of the men of Gibeah, should be followed by a holocaust of dissension and civil war which is not finally worked out until the bones of Saul and his sons are returned to the land of their

26

fathers at 2 Samuel 21.14. Nevertheless the sins of the men of Gibeah are eventually remitted. The sacrifice is not in vain.

But there is much more to it than that, for the story of Gibeah, like the story of Sodom and the story of Noah, is a story about the survival of the virtuous few elected from among the sinful many.

Although this is an audience of Bible readers, I had best remind you of the relevant details.

In the first part of the Gibeah story, a male traveller, the Levite, is offered hospitality by a local citizen, whose house is then surrounded by a mob, who demand that the guest be handed over to them for purposes of homosexual rape, whereupon the host offers instead the sexual services of his virgin daughter. All this is a direct copy of the story of Lot in Sodom (Genesis 19). The only difference is that in the latter there are two travellers, who turn out to be angels, and two virgin daughters. In the Sodom story the daughters are saved because the angels strike the mobsters with blindness; in the Gibeah story the daughter is saved because the traveller offers his concubine as a sacrificial substitute.

But that is not the end of the matter. Sodom is destroyed by God, and Lot and his daughters are the sole survivors. The problem of how the race shall be perpetuated is solved by having the daughters commit incest with their drunken father. From this intercourse are descended the Moabites and the Ammonites.

Gibeah is likewise destroyed along with the whole tribe of Benjamin except for 600 male survivors. The destruction in this case is by human agency. But there is again a problem of the survival of the race, because their fellow Israelites have bound themselves by oath not to marry their daughters to any Benjamite (Judges 21.1). What follows is highly complex. Incest is not involved but the solution entails an irregular form of marriage and the introduction of a further collective mythological entity 'the people of Jabesh-Gilead', whose only function in the biblical texts is to play a punctuating role with respect to the career of Saul.

The people of Jabesh-Gilead are first exterminated so that their surviving virgins shall provide spouses for the surviving Benjamites (Judges 21.12–14). The descendants of this union are the elect of God who provide the first King, Saul (1 Samuel 10.21). Immediately before Saul's final investiture the rehabilitated people of Jabesh-Gilead are besieged by the Ammonites. At the last minute they are rescued by Saul who has mustered his troops by first cutting his plough oxen into pieces and distributing the portions in direct imitation of the Levite's treatment of his dead concubine (1 Samuel 11.7–15).

Finally the men of Jabesh-Gilead recover the dead body of Saul from the Philistines, thereby earning David's commendation (1 Samuel 31.11–13; 2 Samuel 2.4–7). The bones remain in limbo in their charge until the lineage of Saul (with David's collaboration) has been exterminated by the Gideonites and the feud thus brought to an end (2 Samuel 21.14).

Overall, the men of Jabesh-Gilead play a complementary role to the Levite's concubine. The latter takes the story away from Bethlehem in a context of faction and fragmentation; the former brings it back again in a context of reunification. So it is structurally most significant that, whereas the story of David's relationship with Saul starts out with David 'the son of Jesse of Bethlehem' (1 Samuel 17.58) killing the Philistine giant Goliath and then being prevented by Saul from returning to Bethlehem (1 Samuel 18.1–2), the whole complex of stories should end by coming back to just the same point. No sooner have we been told of David's recovery of the bones of Saul and Jonathan from the men of Jabesh-Gilead than we get a listing of the heroic deeds of David and his men. This time it is Elhanan 'son of Jair of Bethlehem' who is credited with the death of Goliath, but it is the Bethlehem reference that is significant; *communitas* has been restored (2 Samuel 21.14–22).

There are many other structuralist points which might be made about this group of stories and I am well aware that I have left all sorts of loose ends hanging in the air. But to tie in all these bits and pieces we should need to consider many additional stories.

Here is one example: the wives who are eventually found for the bereaved Benjamites are proper Israelites but the procedures by which the marriages are arranged are irregular (Judges 21). In the counterpart story of Ruth, which immediately follows, Ruth's marriage to Boaz (which provides heirs to the lineage of Elimelech) is legitimate in form though in order to become so it has to exploit to the full the subtleties of the Israelite law of levirate marriage as specified in Deuteronomy 25.5–10. But in this case, Ruth, being a Moabitess, ought to have been excluded from the congregation (Deuteronomy 23.3). Furthermore, by another line of argument, her marriage must be illegitimate because she is a foreigner (Nehemiah 13.25). Yet it is David and Solomon, the descendants of Ruth, rather than Saul, the descendant of the bereaved Benjamites, who ultimately serve as the paradigm of kingly virtue. Once again we have an association between sacredness and ambiguous marginality.

Please do not misunderstand me. I am not trying to teach the historians their proper business. I have no idea which incidents in the biblical narrative, if any, have some basis in history as it actually happened, and, frankly, I personally am not greatly interested in this issue.

But I insist very strongly that if we are to get at the subliminal, religious, meaning of biblical stories, then they all need to be considered at the same time without consideration of the order in which they appear. They are there in the Bible as we have it today because they were felt to make sense by editors who were sympathetic to Nehemiah's diatribe against the marriage of strange wives (Nehemiah 13.23–31). But these same editors were very sensitive to the close interrelationship between sin and salvation, purity and danger. The religious state of *communitas* lies right on the edge between the permissible and the impermissible. That is what these stories, taken collectively, are really all about.

It is not for me to preach to theologians on such matters, but I do seriously suggest that if you would all forget the purportedly historical frame in which the Bible stories are set, you would find that much that is incomprehensible (the story of the massacre of the Benjamites for example) would begin to make religious sense. In the Middle Ages Christians took one story with another without worrying about chronology or about so-called realism. I believe we should do the same.

Notes

1 Chabrol and Marin (1974) pp. 249–51 has a very valuable bibliography entitled: 'Bibliographie: sémiotique des textes bibliques'. See also the reference in Thiselton (1978) p. 335.
2 *Semeia* is a publication edited in the Department of Religious Studies, University of Montana, Missoula, MT 59812.
3 Rogerson (1978) p. 119.
4 Malinowski's own references to this topic are numerous but scattered, the most immediately relevant is the following quotation which comes from *Myth in Primitive Psychology* (1926) (New York: W. W. Norton) [reprinted in B. Malinowski *Magic, Science and Religion and Other Essays* (1948) and elsewhere]:

Myth ... is not merely a story told but a reality lived. It is not of the nature of fiction, such as we read today in a novel, but it is a living reality, believed to have once happened in primaeval times, and continuing ever since to influence the world and human destinies ... Myth is to the savage, what, to a fully believing Christian, is the Biblical story of the Creation, of the Fall, of the Redemption by Christ's Sacrifice on the Cross. As our sacred story lives in our ritual, in our morality, as it governs our faith and controls our conduct, even so does his myth for the savage.

5 The uncertainty is shared by anthropologists. A striking case is provided by the work of Raphael Patai, who is knowledgeable both as an anthropologist and as a biblical scholar. In Patai (1960) every incident in the biblical narrative is treated as a record of historical fact and as evidence that 'in the days of the Hebrew patriarchs' such and such behaviour was 'a binding custom'. On the other hand Graves and Patai (1964), which is mainly concerned with non-canonical Hebrew sources, includes substantial parts of Genesis under the category myth. Correspondingly the definition of myth

given at Graves and Patai (1964) p. 11 is an uncomfortable compromise between the 'sacred tale' and the 'impossible tale' view.

6 Pitt-Rivers (1977) Chapter 7.
7 For an account of Robertson Smith's career see Beidelman (1974).
8 The passage in question came at p. 393 of Smith (1889). It is quoted at length in Beidelman (1974) p. 57.
9 See reference Frazer (1900).
10 I have in mind Hertz (1907) and Van Gennep (1909). Hertz was Durkheim's pupil. Van Gennep was not actually a member of Durkheim's group but his intellectual stance was very similar.
11 Smith (1889) [3rd Edn (1927) p. 18].
12 See note 4 above.
13 Frankfort (1951).
14 Kitagawa and Long (1969).
15 Morgenstern (1966) p. 6.
16 Douglas (1966) Chapter 3.
17 Douglas (1957).
18 Douglas (1966) p. 54.
19 Douglas (1966) p. 55.
20 Simoons (1961) Chapter 3. It is useless to speculate about the origin of such customs and attitudes. We may note however that if, in a mixed community, one part of the population operates a taboo against pork and another does not then the taboo will function as a badge of ethnic identity. This is in fact what happened in the Israelite/Jewish case.
21 I have not considered in this paper the nature of my disagreement with Pocock (1975) – see above, p. 16. As is apparent from Leach (1969) p. 50, I share Pocock's view that the geography of the Pentateuch has symbolic significance but I do not agree with him that this can be consistently linked with the 'real' cardinal directions of North, South, East, West.
22 Lévi-Strauss (1969).
23 H. H. Koester, the distinguished author of the article on 'Gospels' in the 1969 edition of the *Encyclopaedia Britannica*, asserted without qualification that 'Between Jesus' crucifixion and the first composition of a written gospel at least one generation elapsed.' There are other opinions, e.g. Robinson (1976).
24 Goody (1977) but esp. p. 152.
25 See Leach (1954) pp. 89–100.
26 Turner (1969).

References

Beidelman, T. O. 1974 *W. Robertson Smith and the Sociological Study of Religion*, Chicago: Chicago University Press
Chabrol, C. and Marin, L. 1974 *Le récit évangélique*, Paris: Bibliothèque de Sciences Religieuses
Douglas, M. 1957 'Animals in Lele Religious Symbolism', *Africa*, 24, 3 pp. 214–19
1966 *Purity and Danger. An Analysis of Concepts of Pollution and Taboo*, London: Routledge and Kegan Paul

Eliade, M. 1955 *The Myth of the Eternal Return*, London: Routledge & Kegan Paul, translated from the French edition of 1949

Frankfort, H. 1951 *The Problem of Similarity in Ancient Near Eastern Religions*, Royal Anthropological Institute, The Frazer Lecture for 1951

Frazer, J. G. 1900 'The Crucifixion of Christ', *The Golden Bough* (2nd Edition) Vol. 3 pp. 186–196. Reprinted in 3rd Edition of 1913 as a 'Note' at pp. 412–23 of Part VI The Scapegoat, London: Macmillan

1918 *Folklore in the Old Testament: Studies in Comparative Religion, Legend and Law*, 3 vols, London: Macmillan

Goody, J. 1977 *The Domestication of the Savage Mind*, Cambridge: C.U.P.

Graves, R. and Patai, R. 1964 *Hebrew Myths: The Book of Genesis*, London: Cassell

Hartland, E. S. 1894–6 *The Legend of Perseus*, 3 vols, London: D. Nutt

1909 *Primitive Paternity: The Myth of Supernatural Birth in Relation to the History of the Family*, 2 vols, London: D. Nutt

Hastings, J. (editor) 1909 *Dictionary of the Bible*, Edinburgh: T. & T. Clark

Hertz, R. 1907 'Contribution à une étude sur la représentation collective de la mort', *Année Sociologique*, Vol. x pp. 48–137

Hocart, A. M. 1927 *Kingship*, London: O.U.P.

1936 *Kings and Councillors: An Essay in the Comparative Anatomy of Human Society*, Cairo: Printing Office Paul Barbey, reprint edition edited by R. Needham 1970, Chicago: University of Chicago Press

Hooke, S. H. (editor) 1933 *Myth and Ritual: Essays on the Myth and Ritual of the Hebrews in relation to the Culture Pattern of the Ancient East*, London: O.U.P.

(editor) 1935 *The Labyrinth*, London: O.U.P.

1958 *Myth, Ritual and Kingship: Essays on the Theory and Practice of Kingship in the Ancient Near East and in Israel*, Oxford: Clarendon Press

James, E. O. 1933 *Christian Myth and Ritual: A Historical Study*, London: John Murray

Kitagawa, J. M. and Long, C. H. 1969 *Myths and Symbols: Studies in Honor of Mircea Eliade*, Chicago: University of Chicago Press

Leach, E. (R). 1954 *Political Systems of Highland Burma*, London: Bell [Later editions Athlone Press]

1969 *Genesis as Myth and Other Essays*, London: Cape

1976 *Culture and Communication: The Logic by Which Symbols are Connected*, Cambridge: C.U.P.

Lévi-Strauss, C. (edited by G. Charbonnier) 1969 *Conversations with Claude Lévi-Strauss*, London: Cape

Malinowski, B. 1926 *Myth in Primitive Psychology*, London: Kegan Paul, reprinted in B. Malinowski: *Magic, Science and Religion and Other Essays* (1948), Glencoe Ill.: Free Press

Morgenstern, J. 1966 *Rites of Birth, Marriage, Death and Kindred Occasions among the Semites*, Cincinnati: Hebrew Union College Press

Patai, R. 1960 *Family, Love and the Bible*, London: MacGibbon & Kee

Pitt-Rivers, J. 1977 *The Fate of Shechem or the Politics of Sex*, Cambridge: C.U.P.

Pocock, D. F. 1975 'North and South in the Book of Genesis', in J. H. M. Beattie and R. G. Lienhardt (editors), *Studies in Social Anthropology: Essays in Memory of E. E. Evans-Pritchard by his former Oxford Colleagues*, pp. 273–84 (Oxford: Clarendon Press)

Robertson, J. M. 1911 *Pagan Christs: Studies in Comparative Hierology,* 2nd edition, London: Watts

Robinson, J. A. T. 1976 *Redating the New Testament,* London: SCM Press

Rogerson, J. W. 1978 *Anthropology and the Old Testament,* Oxford: Basil Blackwell

Schapera, I. 1955 'The Sin of Cain' (The Frazer Lecture in Social Anthropology, 1954), *Journal of the Royal Anthropological Insitute,* Vol. 85 pp. 33–43

Schofield, J. N. 1964 *Introducing Old Testament Theology,* London: SCM Press

Simoons, F. J. 1961 *Eat Not This Flesh: Food Avoidances in the Old World,* Madison: University of Wisconsin Press

Smith, W. Robertson 1889 *Lectures on the Religion of the Semites,* 1st Edition (London: A. & C. Black), 2nd edition 1894. 3rd Edition (edited by S. A. Cook) 1927

Thiselton, A. C. 1978 'Structuralism and Biblical Studies: Method or Ideology?', in *The Expository Times,* August 1978 pp. 329–35

Turner, V. W. 1969 *The Ritual Process: Structure and Anti-Structure,* London: Routledge and Kegan Paul

Van Gennep, A. 1909 *Les Rites de passage,* Paris (English edition: *The Rites of Passage,* 1960 (London: Routledge & Kegan Paul)

3 Why did Moses have a sister?*

EDMUND LEACH

Fashions change and even senior members of the present generation of academic anthropologists may be puzzled as to why Thomas Henry Huxley should be honoured by the Institute as if he were the founder ancestor of British anthropology. The explanation is to be found in the obituary published in the *Journal of the Anthropological Institute* in 1896.[1] Huxley was the Leopard Skin Chief who, in 1871, arbitrated between the warring factions of the Ethnological Society and the Anthropological Society and thus established a temporary truce which lasted long enough to get the Anthropological Institute established in its present form. Huxley was not the Noah of British Anthropology but he was perhaps its Moses, its first law-giver.

The Huxley Lecture, with occasional gaps, has been given annually since the beginning of the century. Most, though not all, of the lectures have been published. The earliest examples would have delighted Mr Enoch Powell but do not deserve present day imitation. The first Huxley Lecture to be devoted to a theme falling within the field of social or cultural anthropology was given by Frazer during the First World War. It was a lecture about flood stories and was later published, in expanded form, as part of Chapter 4 of Part I of *Folklore in the Old Testament*[2]. My biblical theme thus has a Frazerian precedent though it will focus around Moses rather than Noah.

When Huxley himself wrote about the Bible it was chiefly in the role of debunker. The Bible stories are in conflict with geological evidence; therefore they are not historical; therefore they are a lot of nonsense. Frazer avoided the 'science *versus* theology' debate and insisted that he was concerned with comparative folklore as an end in itself. My own stance is in no sense anti-religious. I agree with Huxley that the Bible is not true as history, but for the many millions of individuals who consider the Bible to be a sacred tale it is certainly true as myth. I would not wish to challenge that opinion, but the nature of mythical truth is something about which anthropologists have something pertinent to say.

*The Huxley Lecture for 1980

Another preliminary point. The text of the Bible, as we now have it, clearly assumes that the Deity is male. As a general principle there is no obvious reason why a metaphysical First Cause should be endowed with sex or gender at all. On the other hand if God is to be credited with such attributes one might expect that these would somehow combine both male and female qualities. In many highly sophisticated religious systems a balance of this sort is achieved by distributing various aspects of divinity between male gods and female goddesses and then giving mythical sanction to the allocation by associating the goddesses with their male counterparts as mothers, spouses, sisters or daughters. This was the general pattern in the Ancient World both in Mesopotamia and in the Eastern Mediterranean. It is still the general pattern in contemporary India.[3]

And of course, even in Christianity, the presumed masculinity of God is no more than a formula which Christian practice largely ignores.

In the Catholic version, the dogmas by which the human mother of Jesus Christ is declared to be the 'ever Virgin' Queen of Heaven, immaculately conceived of an immaculate mother, has turned her into a goddess in all but name.[4] Conversely, the Protestants, in emphasising the mediating role of the Second Person of the Trinity, have made Him appear markedly effeminate. 'Gentle Jesus, meek and mild' is hardly the paradigm for *machismo*.[5]

During the first three centuries of the Christian era the ambiguity of the sex of the Deity was much more explicit. Some members of my audience will have read Elaine Pagels' recent popular, though scholarly, study of the Nag Hammadi Gnostic gospels.[6] From that account it is plain that, whatever its limitations, Gnostic Christianity would have been highly congenial to contemporary feminists.

In my present lecture I shall only make passing reference to the Gnostic heresies though it is implicit in part of my argument that certain features of the New Testament texts, as we now have them, which have come to seem redundant or even paradoxical, would have been of fundamental importance for the advocates of Gnosticism.

On the other hand the real starting point of my lecture has sometimes been interpreted as a kind of Jewish counterpart to Gnostic Christianity.

The Roman settlement of Dura-Europos in Syria was destroyed by military action in the year A.D. 256. The site was then abandoned. It was excavated from 1927 onwards and in 1932 a large part of the murals on the walls of the obviously prosperous Jewish synagogue were rescued. They are now in Damascus. One of these murals illustrates the

Exodus story of Moses in the Bulrushes. Unexpectedly the picture includes the representation of a goddess. This picture dates from the 3rd Century A.D. and is thus contemporary with the Gnostic heresies of the Christians.[7]

It is this relatively recent period which provides the 'ethnographic present' of my lecture. What I say about Moses and Pharaonic Egypt is not intended to represent history as it actually happened, but mytho-history as it was imagined by the Jews of Dura-Europos and by the Christians of the pre-Constantinian Levant.

That granted I had better start by explaining some of the assumptions that lie at the back of my argument. I take it for granted that none of the stories recorded in the Bible, either in the Old Testament or in the New, are at all likely to be true as history. In its present form the Bible is a much edited compendium of a great variety of ancient documents derived from many different sources, but the end product is a body of mythology, a sacred tale, not a history book.[8] I also take it for granted that when the early Christians described themselves as the New Israel they meant what they said. Their divine law-giver was called Jesus (Joshua) because, like his Old Testament namesake, he was the successor and replacement of Moses.

If you come with me that far then it becomes sensible to ask of any particular incident, either in the Old Testament or in the New, why it is there at all. If the Bible is a mythology it conveys its meaning as a totality, rather after the fashion of a novel by a major novelist; no detail of the plot is there by accident; everything ties in with everything else.

The stories in the Old Testament existed as a cohesive set before the New Testament stories were written at all, but if the New Testament stories represent a more or less conscious transformation of the Old Testament stories, as some texts (e.g. the whole of *The Epistle to the Hebrews*) quite expressly state, then, from a structuralist point of view, the New Testament can illuminate the Old Testament just as the Old Testament illuminates the New. All of which explains why part of my answer to the question: 'Why did Moses have a sister?' is derived from the complementary question: 'Why did Jesus not have a sister?' I am suggesting that we gain insight into the mythological significance of the shadowy women who surround Moses by looking carefully at the significance of the equally shadowy women who surround Jesus.

As Frazer and his contemporaries and many subsequent scholars have demonstrated, many Bible stories have their close parallels in folklore and in other collections of religious literature; I take the existence of such parallels for granted but that is not my present concern. My interest is with the stories as they appear in the Bible, not with alternative versions

35

which may be found elsewhere. I assume that the editor-compilers of the Old and New Testament canon knew what they were up to. They included some stories and some details and rejected others. I assume that the totality of what is included has a meaning and I am interested in that meaning. But I can only hope to get at the meaning by looking at the details of what was included since, for the most part, what was rejected is no longer accessible.[9]

Hence my title. It makes sense to ask why Moses had a sister because, on a first casual reading of the text, Moses' sister Miriam (Mary) seems to be a quite unimportant, almost redundant, figure. So why is she there at all?

One point at least can be taken as self-evident. The central concern of the Bible as a whole is the relationship between God and Man. Before this relationship can be discussed, either in myth or in any other fashion, it must be imagined.

In the course of human history the imaginations of men have credited God with all sorts of physical and metaphysical forms. Even in the Bible there are quite a number, e.g. 'tongues of fire', 'a cloud', 'the Word', 'a still small voice'.[10] But in the Bible the relationship God/Man assumes three predominant forms. I shall call them: (i) the Master/Servant image, (ii) the Kingship image, (iii) the Husband/Wife image. In all three God is anthropomorphic, a magnified non-natural man and unambiguously male. The three images are not mutually exclusive but there are elements of tension between them. Much of the argument of the Bible is taken up with trying to resolve the contradictions in the dialectic which then ensues.

The relational images to which I refer are typified as follows:

1. *Master/Servant*. Here the human servant or bond-slave meets with God, his master, directly face to face, or in a vision, or by inspiration. The servant becomes a prophet. In principle, the ideology is egalitarian; all servants are of the same standing; anyone might become a prophet. In practice, the Grace of God falls only upon the chosen few, the Elect. Moreover, even if all prophets are equal, some are more equal than the others; the principle of equality before God is at odds with the principle of hierarchy. Moses is declared to be superior to Aaron and Miriam because he speaks with God openly 'mouth to mouth', whereas Aaron and Miriam encounter God only in visions and dreams and 'in dark speeches'.[11]

The capacity to prophesy, to act as the mouthpiece of God, is strictly personal; it is not hereditary. Elijah, Ezekiel, John the Baptist are prototype examples. But here too there is tension; the notion that the

36

prophetic role is transmissible creeps in at the corners. Aaron's prophetic role is personal; but his role as high priest is explicitly hereditary.[12] The dying Moses hands on his powers to Joshua who has previously been described as his 'servant, one of his young men';[13] so also Elijah passes on his powers to Elisha;[14] the synoptic gospels momentarily present Jesus as 'John risen from the dead'.[15]

The act of prophecy nearly always takes place in the wilderness or on a river bank away from human habitation – the point being that, in a cosmic sense, such places stand at the boundary between This World and The Other and are therefore appropriate places for a meeting between the natural and the supernatural.[16]

2. *Kingship.* One of the merits of Kingship over other forms of political organisation is that it ensures continuity. Individual kings may die or abdicate or be deposed but the Kingship, as such, is immortal. The living king is simply the temporary holder of an eternal office. Furthermore, since the omnipotence of the living king derives from his office, the office itself possesses two of the major attributes of deity; it is immortal, it is omnipotent. In the outcome, living kings, as delegates of the deity, 'Kingship', have very frequently been worshipped as god incarnate. And this is the case in the Bible.

Both in the Old Testament and in the New, the figure of the Prophet, who is the servant of God, stands opposed to the King who has failed to maintain the moral virtues which are implicit in his role as delegate of God. Yet, in the limiting case, the Prophet himself, the scourge of princes, merges with the ruler who is deity incarnate. Moses, like Jesus Christ, is a god-king as well as a man.[17]

The prototype characteristics of the King are precisely the opposite to those of the Prophet. The Prophet lives an ascetic, solitary life in the wilderness, in mountainous places away from the crowd, dressed in coarse clothing, eating raw, uncooked food – 'locusts and wild honey'; the King lives an erotic life, surrounded by women and courtiers, in a palace in the city, dressed in fine raiment, feasting sumptuously.[18] But correspondingly, in the context of Kingship, God ceases to be a burning bush in the 'backside of the desert'[19] and becomes a kind of super-king with his residence in the Holy of Holies of the Temple, at the centre of the Holy City, at the centre of the Holy Land.[20]

Although the roles of Prophet and King are radically opposed, any particular character in the story may, and very frequently does, occupy both roles at different stages of his or her career. For example the first half of Exodus Chapter 2 links Moses with Kingship; he becomes the adopted son of Pharaoh's daughter. But the second half of the chapter, together with Chapter 3, takes him into the wilderness where he becomes son-in-law to the Priest of Midian and communes directly with God who appears to him as a flame of fire in 'the Mountain of God'. And so also with Saul. He is anointed as future King 'in the city',[21] but a little later he is in a state of ecstasy among a company of prophets who have just come down from the high place which is 'the hill of God'.[22] Similarly the anointing of David as King takes place in cities, first in Bethlehem, then in Hebron;[23] but he is a shepherd in the wilderness before he gets mixed up with the city business of Kingship at all.[24]

We meet with just the same pattern in the New Testament. Matthew 2 tells us that Jesus was born in Bethlehem to be the divine King,[25] but then in Matthew 3 Jesus becomes inspired by the Spirit of God at the hands of John the Baptist on the banks of the Jordan.[26] In this prophetic state he then goes out into the Wilderness to argue with the Devil.[27] Likewise in the epiphany when the disciples see Jesus walking upon the sea. He has first performed the miracle of feeding the five thousand in 'a desert place' and then gone up into 'a mountain to pray'.[28] The comparable feeding of the four thousand is also 'in the wilderness' and is followed by the Transfiguration which occurs on 'a high mountain apart'.[29] But when Matthew reverts to the theme of Jesus as King, the setting is the city of Jerusalem with Jesus ordering people about and treating his disciples as servants, while acting as if the Temple were his personal palace.[30]

In general, the Kingship image represents God as an all powerful but somewhat remote ruler who can only be approached through inter-mediaries such as living priests and deceased saints. In contrast to the Master/Servant image, which fits with a pentecostal ideology and an egalitarian, congregationalist type of church-organisation, the Kingship pattern is systematically hierarchical. In Christianity this latter aspect of Deity is given special emphasis in Roman Catholicism and in episco-palian forms of Protestantism. The Lord God is 'King of Kings, the only ruler of Princes'.[31]

In constructing an image of divine kingship the original authors of the books which now make up the Old Testament might have drawn on a variety of actual human institutions. In the Pentateuch the model that was actually used was that of the Egyptian Pharaoh. In Egyptian myth-ology and religious practice the Pharaoh was treated as a divine king in a quite explicit sense. The fact that certain of the Patriarchs, in particular Abraham, Joseph, and Moses, are, by different devices, identified with Pharaoh, thus carries the implication that they are not just representa-tives of God but, in some degree, God incarnate in their own persons. This was an accepted part of Jewish tradition which is reflected in the incident where Luke represents Abraham as a kind of Osiris figure, ruler of the Land of the Dead.[32]

Please try to understand my argument. I am treating the biblical texts as mythology not as history. I am not following in the footsteps of Hocart and S. H. Hooke in supposing that, at some uncertain date towards the end of the second millennium B.C., a single pattern of Kingship, for which Egypt provided the prototype, prevailed throughout the Middle East.[33] What I am talking about are the images of Jewish antiquity which coloured the thinking of Jews who were the contemporaries of Josephus.

Furthermore, in saying that, in the texts, certain of the patriarchs are 'identified with Pharaoh', I am not suggesting that the Jews simply borrowed their religious ideas from the Egyptians. It is rather that the religious ideology surrounding the real Pharaoh, during the relatively late Hellenic period, embodied, in a highly condensed form, a particular structure of religious ideas. Permuted forms of this same structure appear as episodes in the Bible. But, both at the level of manifest plot and at the level of structural pattern, the Jewish and Christian versions are *transformations* of the Egyptian version. Cultural borrowing is not the simple piecemeal process which scholars of Frazer's generation argued about, and, although Hocart and his friend Lord Raglan were structuralists in embryo, I am not here simply recapitulating what they were saying nearly fifty years ago.[34]

So let us take a closer look at the relationship between the stories about the patriarchs as they appear in Genesis and Exodus and the stereotyped late form of the saga of Osiris.

(i) *Abraham*. In ancient times, as in modern, one of the best known legends concerning the Egyptian kingship was that the principal wife of the Pharaoh was a sister or half-sister.[35] This practice (in so far as it really took place) was modelled upon a celebrated mythological formula. In myth, the god Osiris is married to his sister the goddess Isis and is 'killed' by his brother Seth; the god Horus is the son of Osiris and Isis but posthumously conceived. The living Pharaoh of Egypt was treated as an incarnation of Horus; his predecessor was worshipped as an incarnation of Osiris. In mytho-logic the Queen mother and the Queen sister-wife were both representations of Isis. In anthropological jargon, the structural pattern, at the mythological level, was one of 'positional succession based on sibling incest'. The pattern is illustrated schematically in my Fig. 1.

In our biblical texts the assimilation of Abraham to the Pharaonic model and hence to the Osiris–Horus schema of positional succession is fairly straightforward. Abraham's principal wife of Sarah was his half-sister.[36] The name Sarah means 'princess'; it has recently been suggested that it may have phonetic and historical links with Hera,[37] who appears in Greek mythology as the principal wife of the supreme deity Zeus. In Genesis 12

Sarah becomes a minor wife of Pharaoh; the plain implication of the story is that Pharaoh and Abraham are virtually interchangeable.[38]

Sarah is taken to wife by Pharaoh because she is very beautiful; she was also, by implication, at least sixty-five years old.[39] If Sarah is viewed as a real person such discrepancies have to be explained away; if she is a mythological transformation of Isis there is no problem.

In slightly different versions of the same story Abraham's sister-wife Sarah is taken to wife by Abimelech, King of Gerah,[40] while Isaac, the son of Abraham, describes his wife Rebekah as his sister even though she is not,[41] seemingly in anticipation that she likewise will be taken to wife, either by the same Abimelech or by one of his people. The name Abimelech means 'father is King'.[42]

(ii) *Joseph*. Abraham and Sarah are brought into contact with Pharaoh in Egypt because Abraham has gone South into Egypt to avoid famine in the Land of Canaan (Palestine).[43] This polarity, in which the opposition

(i) Basic formula:—

"If God the Father and God the Son are consubstantial co-eternal, then 'the mother of God' is also 'the spouse of God' and the mother is spouse to her own son

(ii) In diagram form this reads:—

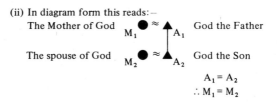

The Mother of God M_1 ≈ A_1 God the Father

The spouse of God M_2 ≈ A_2 God the Son

$$A_1 = A_2$$
$$\therefore M_1 = M_2$$

(iii) The relationship between the male aspect of deity A and the female aspect of deity M may then be viewed either as mother/son, or wife/husband, or daughter/father, or sister/brother. The Osiris, Isis, Horus mythology combines all these possibilities

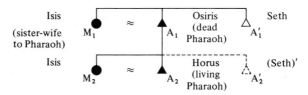

Isis (sister-wife to Pharaoh) M_1 ≈ A_1 Osiris (dead Pharaoh) A_1' Seth

Isis M_2 ≈ A_2 Horus (living Pharaoh) A_2' (Seth)'

Figure 1. Positional succession in Egyptian kingship.

40

Palestine/Egypt is made to stand for the opposition 'Land of Famine and Suffering' / 'Land of Plenty and Safety', appears again in many biblical stories, though sometimes the values are reversed. Thus in Exodus it is Palestine that stands for Plenty and Egypt for Suffering, but the Christian story[44] repeats the Genesis version in which Egypt stands for Safety and Palestine for Danger and Suffering. In all versions the polar geographical categories, (1) 'Egypt' – (2) 'Palestine' are separated by an intermediate category 'The Wilderness'. Furthermore, in the lead story of Exodus, the transition from Egypt to Wilderness and from Wilderness to Palestine are both marked by the magical crossing of a water boundary on dry land.[45] Here, as elsewhere, the biblical Wilderness is a zone of liminality in Victor Turner's sense.[46] It is this intermediate region which provides the location for 'the mountain of God' and it is here that Moses and his companions converse directly with Deity.

The Joseph story repeats the Abraham pattern. Joseph, who is the favourite son of his patriarch father Jacob-Israel, grandson of Abraham, arrives in Egypt in the status of a Midianite slave as a consequence of his having boasted to his half-brothers that he had dreamed that he would become a King and would rule over them. In Egypt Joseph becomes the slave of Potiphar, 'an officer of Pharaoh', and he successfully resists the seductions of Potiphar's wife.[47] Later in the story, after he has become Pharaoh's Viceroy, Pharaoh gives him as wife 'Asenath, the daughter of Potiphera, priest of On.'[48] Potiphar and Potiphera are alternative spellings of the same name.[49] Notice that it is Pharaoh, not Potiphera, who exercises the rights of a father over Asenath. Asenath is the mother of Joseph's sons Ephraim and Manasseh.[50]

The structure of this story can be fitted directly to Fig. 1 on the basis of the following equations, all of which are implicit in the biblical text:

Potiphar = 'an officer of' Pharaoh = Pharaoh = (Osiris)
Potiphar's wife = Pharaoh's wife . . . . = (Isis)
Asenath = Potiphera's daughter = Pharaoh's daughter = (Isis)
Joseph = Pharaoh's (adopted) son = (Horus)

It was a well known practice in Ancient Egypt for an elderly Pharaoh to establish his son and heir as co-ruler. It would seem that the senior Pharaoh then ranked as Osiris and the junior as Horus. The biblical Pharaoh establishes Joseph as his co-ruler in just this fashion.[51]

It follows that when Joseph's brethren travel down to Egypt because of famine in Palestine they are recapitulating the earlier journey of Abraham on his visit to Pharaoh. The myth is again affirming that the ruler of Israel is a Pharaoh, a deity incarnate.

(iii) *David and Solomon.* We meet with the same themes in later biblical

41

contexts. Solomon becomes co-ruler with David before the death of the latter[52] and the very first thing that is reported after 'the kingdom was established in the hand of Solomon' is that Solomon marries Pharaoh's daughter.[53] Solomon is the son of Bath-Sheba ('daughter of Sheba') a lady improperly seduced by David before he marries her.[54] Later Solomon is visited by the Queen of Sheba, whom Josephus describes as 'Queen of Egypt and Ethiopia'.[55] According to Ethiopian legend Solomon married the Queen of Sheba and her descendants became Kings of Ethiopia. There is also the story by which Abishag the Shunammite first becomes a virgin spouse to David in his extreme old age.[56] Thereafter the issue as to whether Solomon or one of his brothers shall finally succeed to the Kingship is made to turn upon a dispute as to who shall inherit the virgin Abishag.[57]

Here once again Fig. 1 fits the story with little distortion:

David = Senior Pharaoh = (Osiris)
Bath-Sheba = Queen of Sheba = Abishag = (Isis)
Solomon = Junior Pharaoh = (Horus)

(iv) *Moses*. The Moses story starting from Exodus 2 represents a more complicated transformation of the Osiris–Isis–Horus pattern. The nature of this transformation can be seen by comparing my Fig. 1 with Fig. 2. Since Moses is the adopted son of Pharaoh's daughter the schema of Fig. 1 would imply that Moses' father should be the equivalent of the husband of Pharoah's daughter [A2 in the diagram]. However, since M1 = M2 = Isis, who is sister to A1, A2 is married to his father's sister. Now in the biblical text we are given the apparently gratuitous information that Moses' mother Jochabed was father's sister to his father Amram,[58] implying a marriage which was incestuous according to the formal rules.[59] In terms of the model schema, this makes Moses the structural equivalent of his own father [see Fig. 2: Moses (A″3) = Amram (A3); Jochabed (M2′) = Pharaoh's daughter' (M2)]. If we pursue this line of equivalences and treat Fig. 2 as a variation of Fig. 1, then all the 'M' characters are representations of Isis while all the 'A' characters are alternating representations of Osiris–Horus. Hence both Jochabed and her daughter Miriam equate with Isis.

Those of you who are unfamiliar with structuralist games of this sort will probably find this rather far-fetched, but the reductionism makes sense of a number of other puzzling details.

Thus in the story of Moses in the bulrushes[60] the characters 'Pharaoh's daughter', 'the child's sister', 'the child's mother' are all unnamed but the sister is seemingly redundant. Moreover the very existence of a sister is anomalous since it has just been implied that Moses is Jochabed's first

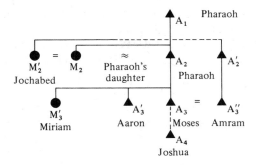

(i) Moses is biological son of Jochabed and Amram
(ii) Moses is adopted son of Pharaoh's daughter
(iii) Moses is sibling to Aaron and Miriam
(iv) Joshua is successor to Moses by election and not by genealogy

As in Fig. 1. All the males (A) are equivalent
All the females (M) are equivalent

Figure 2. Exodus transformation of Egyptian prototype.

born child.[61] But in fact the mother and the sister play slightly different roles. The mother hides the child; the sister observes the discovery. It is a story about death and rebirth with a change of witnesses in between, and, as we shall see presently, this is a crucial feature of the biblical versions of the story.

In the Egyptian original it is Osiris who dies at the hand of Seth. The loving sister-wife Isis then reassembles the dismembered parts of Osiris' body and becomes pregnant by her dead husband-brother. From this pregnancy of a 'Virgin' mother is born Horus. The infant is hidden in the reeds of the Nile Delta to evade the vengeance of Seth. Horus is Osiris reborn.[62]

But if the 'infant Moses in the bulrushes' equates with the 'infant Horus in the reeds', then the Pharaoh who orders the midwives to kill the male children of the Hebrews is Seth, the usurper King, brother, murderer and perpetual enemy of Osiris–Horus.

The whole pattern reappears in the New Testament story of the birth of Jesus. The King Herod who orders the massacre of the innocents is a close copy of the Pharaoh of Exodus Chapter 1.[63] Furthermore, if we follow the lead of Christian artists down the centuries and transform the 'wise men' of Matthew Chapter 2, together with the Shepherds of Luke Chapter 2, into 'three Kings'[64] then the 'babe lying in a manger' discovered by the Kings equates with the baby lying in 'an ark of bulrushes' discovered by a Princess. Notice that both the Kings and the Princess

43

arrive on the scene as emissaries of Seth (Herod in the one case; Pharaoh in the other). So Jesus, like Moses, is a Horus figure and we are led to start thinking about possible connections between Mary (Miriam), the virgin mother of Jesus, and Miriam, the virgin sister of Moses, and the archetypal figure of Isis who manages to be mother, sister, wife, daughter all at once.

Incidentally, in the Exodus story, the long sequence of contests between Moses and Pharaoh which lead to the plagues of Egypt[65] is strongly reminiscent of the Egyptian story known as *The Contendings of Horus and Seth* in that, in each individual contest, Horus (Moses) successfully vanquishes the usurper Seth (Pharaoh), but the battle then immediately starts all over again. This should not surprise us for, in the language of myth, if this were not the case time would come to a full stop. In myth there can be no finality.

Likewise, in myth, it is a marker of sanctity that the Hero should be seen to break the rules of society with impunity. This is the case with the patriarchs. Abraham is married to his half-sister contrary to the rules of incest; Joseph marries an Egyptian contrary to the rules of endogamy; Amram breaks the rules of incest; Moses twice breaks the rules of endogamy, first by marriage to Zipporah, the daughter of Jethro 'the priest of Midian',[66] secondly by marriage to an unnamed Ethiopian.[67]

	Land of Suffering	WILDERNESS (betwixt and between)	Land of Plenty
ABRAHAM	PALESTINE	Instructs Sarah to say she is ⟶ Abraham's sister	EGYPT Sarah marries Pharaoh who is thereby contaminated
• JOSEPH		Has visions. Prophesies, becomes ⟶ Midianite slave	Becomes deputy of Pharaoh and son-in-law of deputy Pharaoh
MOSES	EGYPT	becomes Son-in-law of Midianite Priest and communes ⟶ directly with God	PALESTINE [does not reach promised land but succession passes to Joshua who does]

Figure 3

Fig. 3 pulls together some of the argument so far. It emphasises the geographic frame of reference. It exhibits Joseph and Moses as complementary characters. Both are directly linked with Pharaoh; both have a dual role as secular ruler and as inspired prophet; the latter role of prophet is linked with the liminal 'Wilderness' situation. But the two characters move in opposite directions: Joseph from Palestine to Egypt, Moses from Egypt towards Palestine.

(v) *Miriam.* What then of Moses' sister? Why all the fuss? What is there special about Miriam anyway? But that precisely is the point. There is nothing special about Miriam and that is the puzzle.

As in a novel, characters in myth are not there just by accident as decorations to the story; they have meaning. In Bible stories female characters may be introduced in order to act as sacred mothers to sacred heirs, e.g. Sarah, Rebekah, Rachel, the Canaanitess Tamar, the Moabitess Ruth, Bath-Sheba, the Virgin Mary;[68] or to suffer dishonour and thereby cause a feud, e.g. Dinah, who cohabited with a Shechemite Prince, and Tamar,[69] the sister of Absalom, who was raped by her half-brother Amnon,[70] or to play an heroic role, e.g. Deborah,[71] or a manifestly evil role, e.g. Jezebel,[72] or for a variety of other role-playing reasons; but Miriam hardly seems to have any role at all. Yet in Jewish tradition Miriam was rated as one of the leaders of the Exodus, along with her siblings Moses and Aaron.[73] And of course, if my Horus analogy is valid, and Moses is the god-king of Exodus 7.1, who can Miriam be but the goddess-queen? But how is it worked out?

Apart from cross-references, Miriam appears in the text on only four occasions. These are:

(i) in the story of Moses in the bulrushes where, as we have seen, she is unnamed and mixed up with Jochabed, also unnamed, and Pharaoh's daughter.

(ii) in Exodus 15.20–1 where she is named and described as 'the prophetess, the sister of Aaron'.

(iii) in Numbers 12 where she is stricken with leprosy after having the temerity to complain about Moses' irregular marriage to an Ethiopian. In this case Miriam is apparently punished for having claimed that, being a prophetess, she was the equal to Moses, whereas God here defends the principle of hierarchy. Moses is altogether special. Miriam repents. She is (by implication) cured at Moses' request. But she is then required to undergo a purification ritual lasting seven days.

(iv) at Numbers 20.1 which reports her death. This comes immediately after a statement of the rules that are to be imposed on those who have had contact with a dead body.[74] Whatever else she may be, this Old Testament Miriam (Mary) is very much a tabooed person and in this respect at least she is an appropriate forerunner of her various New Testament successors.

Of the latter it first deserves note that while it can be held that the Gospels refer to a number of different Marys, several of them are very much mixed up, and we are not straying into heresy if we make up a composite figure out of Mary, the sister of Martha and Lazarus, who annoints Jesus' feet with precious ointments in the house of Simon the Leper, and the Mary who performs a similar act in the house of Simon the Pharisee. From a very early date this latter Mary has been identified with Mary Magdalene so that, throughout the Christian era, Mary Magdalene has been seen as the prototype of a repentant prostitute.[75]

If you follow up the cross-references you will see that this composite Mary is, like Miriam, a repentant sinner associated with leprosy and also, like Isis, associated with death and resurrection. Furthermore this Mary is said to be 'loved' by Jesus.[76] In the Bible the nature of this love is not explained but in the Gnostic texts a bond of erotic love links Jesus with Mary Magdalene.[77]

These traditionally established identifications cannot be justified from a strict reading of the canonical text though they fit perfectly with structuralist arguments. Thus whereas Mary, the sister of Martha, is witness to the resurrection of her brother Lazarus,[78] Mary Magdalene is the principal witness of the resurrection of Jesus. In the mythic structure they are one and the same. On the other hand Mary, the Virgin, the mother of Jesus, has just the opposite characteristics. She is sinless and sexless instead of sinful and sexual; she is the vehicle of birth rather than the witness of resurrection, that is of rebirth.

I shall be returning to this mix-up of New Testament Marys presently.

As we have seen already, despite lack of biblical authority, artistic tradition has turned the witnesses to Christ's Nativity into three Kings. This lies within a convention which seems to derive from classical sources whereby the witnesses to a miraculous birth should be three gift-bearing Graces.[79] Thus my next illustration (Plate 1) illustrates the immaculate birth of the Virgin Mary. And this at last brings us back to Dura-Europos. The murals as they now stand in Damascus have been considerably altered by indiscreet 'restoration'. However my illustration (Plate 2) derives from a drawing which was made immediately after the excavation in 1932 and before the restorers had got to work.[80]

The scene depicts the story of Moses in the bulrushes. A substantial section bottom right is missing. The original is strongly coloured. The usual interpretation is:

(a) The enthroned figure on the right is Pharaoh giving orders to the midwives to destroy the boy infants.

46

(b) The standing figures at the centre are the midwives. However they are not the midwives who are named in the text but Jochabed and Miriam posing as midwives.[81]

(c) The kneeling figure below cannot be firmly identified but might be the Princess discovering the ark containing the infant Moses.

(d) The two figures far left are dressed in exactly the same costumes as the midwives at centre and are evidently the same characters over again. They are interpreted as Jochabed and Miriam holding the infant Moses who has a face.

(e) In the water below is the ark, which, instead of having the appearance of a basket of bulrushes, looks like a miniature Roman sarcophagus.

(f) The naked female rising from the water and holding a faceless infant has no obvious counterpart in the text but her iconography is clearly identified by the locket she is wearing round her neck and by her full frontal exposure. She is a goddess named Anahita, who is a transform of Aphrodite (see Plate 3).[82]

(g) Behind Anahita stand three female figures bearing treasures. They are three Graces attending as witnesses to a miraculous birth, or rather to a miraculous rebirth. This is a scene of resurrection from the dead.

The number three is recurrent. On the right the unidentified woman kneels in the water in front of the 'midwives'; on the left the goddess stands in the water in front of Jochabed and Miriam. If, as the costumes imply, the midwives are also Jochabed and Miriam then the kneeling figure should be the equivalent of the goddess. Since the Princess, the daughter of Pharaoh, must be in the picture somewhere, it is plausible that the kneeling figure is in fact the Princess and that she is represented as a transform of the goddess of love. This makes excellent sense if she were considered to be an incarnation of Isis.[83]

I appreciate that this may be beginning to look very Frazerian but let me remind you that my ethnographic present is the third Century A.D., a period at which the international Romanised cult of Isis was at its peak.

The various mother goddesses of the Ancient Civilisations were not as interchangeable as Frazer suggested but by this late date they were not clearly distinguished. Egyptian figures of Isis and Horus of this period are easily mistaken for later figures of the Christian Virgin and Child. In antiquity, in her alternative forms of Hathor and Sothis, Isis had close links with both the sky and the waters of the Nile. In one of the very early Coffin Texts the son of Isis proclaims:

> My mother Isis suckled me. I tasted her sweetness...
> I am the babe of the primaeval waters...[84]

Here surely, in this Dura mural, is just such a babe of the primaeval waters.

Again, in her star form, Isis was Sothis, the Dog Star, whose rising in the East just before dawn heralded the annual inundation and the rebirth of vegetation.[85] Don't jump to conclusions; I am not suggesting that, at the end of the day, all Old and New Testament Miriams can be explained away as vegetation goddesses, but the Star of Bethlehem, which guides the Magi to the place of Jesus' birth and which has now established itself firmly in the iconography of our commercialised Christmas, could very well be an echo of Isis' stellar transformation.

But now I must take a different track.

3. *Husband/Wife.* Right at the beginning I cited the Husband/Wife image as a third major biblical representation of the relationship between God and Man. Let me elaborate that thesis.

The Song of Songs (Canticles) consists of a somewhat jumbled sequence of poems all of which are very explicitly concerned with marriage and the joys of sexual intercourse. Down the centuries many of the more prudish theologians, Jewish as well as Christian, have expressed astonishment that such a document should form part of the orthodox canon; but there it is. The Christian explanation is that the bridegroom–lover–prince is Jesus Christ in his divine manifestation, while the bride–princess is the Church as a collectivity. The same imagery appears in other parts of the Bible, e.g. in Ezekiel and Hosea,[86] where the love of God for the people of Israel is seen as the love of a bridegroom for his bride, while the subsequent unfaithfulness of the Israelites is denounced as 'whoredom'.

Incidentally Canticles brings out very clearly the fact, recently elaborated by Marcel Detienne, that in the Hellenistic World 'frankincense and myrrh' were considered to be prototypical aphrodisiacs.[87] Why then did the witnesses to Christ's Nativity bear gifts of frankincense and myrrh?[88] Were they attending a birth or a wedding? Perhaps the right answer is: 'both'.

In Christianity the imagery is explicit. Not only is the Holy Ghost of the Annunciation a kind of bridegroom to the Virgin Mary, but, in subsequent Catholic Christian practice the Virgin becomes the Shulamite of Canticles who originated as the Abishag whom we have met with already. In this form, the Virgin is not just the Heavenly Queen Mother: she is the Bride of Christ. And in succession to the Virgin in this capacity, every Roman Catholic nun, who formally takes the veil, is a Bride of Christ. Indeed every girl at her first communion is similarly a Bride of Christ.[89] We are back again with a symbolism in which the roles of mother, wife, sister, daughter all merge into a single person.

This switching of roles between being mother and bride to the incarnate Deity already makes the Virgin Mary of Christian story a kind of Isis is a rather simple sense, but the total system of inter-connected tales is much more complicated than that.

Let us take a closer look at the gospel stories which report the witnesses to the crucifixion and the resurrection. The latter are usually grouped in threes and a number of them are called Mary (Miriam).

The chart [Fig. 4] summarises the various statements on the subject. I distinguish between the named witnesses at the Cross, i.e. witnesses to the death, and named witnesses at the empty tomb, i.e. witnesses to the resurrection or rebirth.

Matthew 27.56. At the Cross
(1) M. Magdalene; (2) M. 'the mother of James and Joseph'; (3) 'the mother of Zebedee's children'
Matthew 27.61. At the Tomb
(1) M. Magdalene; (2) 'the other Mary'
Mark 15.40. At the Cross
(1) M. Magdalene; (2) M. 'the mother of James the Younger and Joseph'; (3) Salome
Mark 15.47. At the Tomb (the Deposition)
(1) M. Magdalene; (2) M. 'the mother of Joseph'
Mark 16.1. At the Tomb (the Resurrection)
(1) M. Magdalene; (2) M. 'the mother of James'
(3) Salome
Luke 23.49–56 At the Cross & at the Tomb (the Deposition)
(1) unnamed 'women from Galilee'
(2) Joseph of Arimathaea
Luke 24.10 At the Tomb (the Resurrection)
(1) M. Magdalene; (2) Joanna; (3) M. 'the mother of James' [(4) at v. 12 Peter]
John 19.25 At the Cross
(1) 'his mother'; (2) 'his mother's sister'
(3) M. 'the wife of Clopas'; (4) M. Magdalene
John 19.38–42 At the Tomb (the Deposition)
(1) Joseph of Arimathaea; (2) Nicodemus
John 20.1 At the Tomb (the Resurrection)
(1) M. Magdalene; (2) 'the disciple whom Jesus loved' (3) Simon Peter
John 20.11–12 At the Tomb (the Resurrection)
(1) Magdalene; (2, 3) 'two angels in white'

Fig. 4 The last witnesses at the Cross and the first witnesses to the Resurrection. [M. = Mary]

Several features of these lists bear upon my argument: (1) It is very striking that, despite other variations, Mary Magdalene, who is otherwise a shadowy figure, invariably appears as the principal witness to the Resurrection. (2) By contrast, Mary, the mother of Jesus, is only mentioned once; she is a witness to the death on the Cross but not to the Resurrection. (3) A number of the stated relationships are ambiguous. Thus it has recently been pointed out that the reference in Luke 24 to 'Mary the mother of James' might alternatively be to the 'wife' or 'daughter' of James.[90] (4) The woman listed in Mark 16 are said to have brought spices (in Greek myron = myrrh) to anoint the dead body even though the tomb was already sealed. Luke (23.56–24.1) gives a similar story for the women listed at Luke 24.10. Comparably in John 19.40 Joseph of Arimathaea and Nicodemus wrap myrrh into the linen in which the dead body of Jesus is shrouded when it is placed in the tomb. This is said to be a Jewish burial custom but I have not discovered independent evidence for such a practice. Such embalming of a corpse seems, on the face of it, very Egyptian but this is an odd context in which to encounter an aphrodisiac.

Ordinary Jewish graves of this period were holes in the ground sealed by a stone slab though a few high-status individuals were buried in rock hewn caves. Some of the examples illustrated by Goodenough would fit well with the biblical account.[91] Joseph of Arimathaea has clearly been introduced into the story so that Jesus should have a tomb appropriate to his divine king status. But in John 11.38 Lazarus is also buried in a cave which on the face of it seems quite inappropriate.

The variations in the lists are also interesting. Where Mark has Salome, Luke has Joanna. Who are these people? In the only other reference Joanna appears as a kind of *alter* of Mary Magdalene:

> certain women, which had been healed of evil spirits and infirmities, Mary called Magdalene, out of whom went seven devils, and Joanna, wife of Chuza, Herod's steward...

Is this an echo of Potiphar's wife, the wife of Pharaoh's steward? Or an echo of Miriam cured of leprosy by Moses?

On the face of it Salome must be the same as the mother of James and John 'the sons of Zebedee' who were also called 'Boanerges' – 'the sons of thunder',[92] a title which Christians of the first Century A.D. would surely have taken to imply kinship with Zeus–Jupiter, the thunderer King of Heaven? But why should she be called Salome?

According to Josephus the 'daughter of Herodias' was so named, and it has been a part of Christian tradition since the earliest times that the virgin girl who danced before Herod (thus behaving like a temple prostitute) and received as reward the head of John the Baptist[93] was called Salome. So Mark's Salome and Luke's Joanna as witnesses to the Resurrection both suggest a cross-reference to Herod's Palace and the death of John the Baptist, the Prophet forerunner of Jesus himself. But furthermore, if the stories in Matthew, Mark and John are all put together, then the Salome who is the mother of 'the sons of thunder' becomes the sister of the Virgin Mary.[94]

A parallel set of ambiguities[95] surrounds the various individuals named James in the New Testament. There is James the son of Zebedee, who is, according to the above reckoning, mother's sister's son to Jesus; there is James 'the brother of Joses (Joseph)' whose mother is called Mary and is (in Mark) a witness to the Resurrection alongside Mary Magdalene; there is James 'the Lord's brother', who appears in St Paul's epistles as head of the Church in Jerusalem.[96] According to legend this last James was martyred by being thrown from the pinnacle of the Temple.[97]

As in the Gospel text which provides the model for this story,[98] James was preserved from death as if he were the Son of God, though afterwards he was killed by stoning and beating with a fuller's club.

James, that is Jacob, is a notably appropriate name for the ancestral founder of a church which proclaimed itself to be 'the New Israel' through I agree that somewhere in the Epistles and Acts, myth and legend must merge with history as it actually happened. All the same, in terms of my general argument, it is surely very remarkable that this presumably historical James should have been credited with such a structurally entangled pedigree, linking him closely not only with Jesus (Joshua), the divine Son, the heavenly King, and the latter's mother, the para-divine Mary (Miriam), the heavenly Queen, but also, by a kind of side-step, with John, the Prophet of the Wilderness. And here we need to remember that where Jesus was the son of Mary, a youthful Virgin, John was the son of Elizabeth, a barren woman, 'well stricken in years'[99] and that, by one account, Mary and Elizabeth were 'cousins'.[100]

My Fig. 5, like my earlier Fig. 2, is a transform of the original Fig. 1 which displayed the Osiris–Horus–Isis myth as a schema of positional succession. Here the schema is adapted to the New Testament data which I have just mentioned. As before the M. characters on the left can all be seen as representations of Isis while the A. figures on the right are alternating representations of Osiris and Horus.

Art and legend have gone beyond the text in attempting to iron out the inconsistencies. Although early Christian art sometimes depicted Joseph as a young man in the prime of life a very early apocryphal literature turned him into an old man (A1′), past the age of sexual vigour, with a

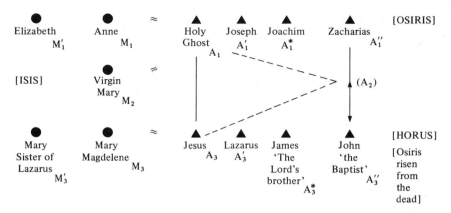

Figure 5. New Testament transformation of the positional succession model.

young wife (M2), thus reversing the generational asymmetry of the Jochabed/Amram story. In the text the youthful Mary (M2) and the aged Elizabeth (M1') are 'cousins' but legend provided Mary with parents, Joachim and Anne, and an immaculate conception. Thereafter the Holy Family of medieval and Renaissance art becomes confused. The aged non-biblical Anne (M1) is mixed up with the aged biblical Elizabeth (M1'). Joseph (A1') merges with both Joachim (A1*) and Zacharias (A1''). Schematically, Mary the Virgin (M2) is left as an anomaly. She is a generation senior to Jesus (A3), Lazarus (A3') James (A3*) and John (A3'') but a generation junior to all the other male characters. Further since Lazarus, in his death and resurrection, is the *alter* of Jesus, the other Marys in the diagram, Mary Magdalene (M3) and Mary 'the sister of Lazarus' (M3'), are both a generation junior to Mary (M2). The ambiguity of M2's age status is of course the mythical crux.

(vi) *Ashtoreth*. The next step in my analysis takes us further back into antiquity. But remember again the two infants in the Dura mural; the one with a face, which is held joyfully by its mother and the one without a face which seems just to have been lifted from a sarcophagus floating in the river.

The religious ideology of the Old Testament was developed in a geographical context in which the sacrifice of firstborn children was very widespread. There are scores of biblical references to these practices which are confirmed by archaeology.[101] They were associated with a cult in which deity was viewed as having two aspects, one male and one female. The male deity was a King (the biblical Melech, Molech,

Moloch); the female deity was a mother-goddess Queen (Ishtar, Astarte etc... the biblical Ashtaroth). Sixty years ago Nicholas König, a semitic scholar at Columbia University, summarised her characteristics in Frazerian language as:

> The goddess of fertility, productiveness and love on the one hand, and of war, death and decay on the other, a personification of the earth as it passes through the summer and winter seasons.[102]

Indologists will perhaps find it simpler to see this goddess as a combination of Parvati and Kali. Such generalisations doubtless oversimplify the facts but that is the pattern.[103]

Jewish reformers, as represented in the story of King Josiah,[104] repeatedly sought to distance themselves from the 'abominations' of this Moloch/Ashtoreth cult in two particular respects:– (1) they insisted the God is exclusively male; (2) they endeavoured to replace the institution of child sacrifice by alternative practices.

Broadly speaking I agree with Frazer[105] that the underlying rationale of child sacrifice is that a birth which 'opens the womb' is a mystical, contaminating event which puts in danger not only the mother but all the senior members of her household, including the mother's future unborn children. In the Genesis stories the firstborn son is not killed but he is deprived of his birthright. When Hagar gives birth to Ishmael she is deputising for her barren mistress Sarah, but later Ishmael is cast out *into the wilderness* in favour of the sacred heir Isaac.[106] Likewise Esau, the elder of Rebekah's twin sons, is cast out in favour of Jacob,[107] and then there is the strange story of the birth of the twins Pharez and Zarah. Although Pharez is born first it is Zarah who 'opens the womb'. Pharez is the sacred heir.[108]

Comparably in the David and Bath Sheba story, the death of Bath Sheba's firstborn child removes the contamination of sin and thereby preserves the life of both David and of the future child Solomon, the sacred heir.[109]

In all these stories there is a recurrent theme of replacement. The sacred heir is a replacement of a contaminated child. The replacement belongs to God; the contaminated child is taken by Azazel, the ambiguous Spirit of the Wilderness.[110] But although the contaminated children were rejected they were not killed.

The biblical Israelites, as described in the Pentateuch, retained the custom of sacrifice of the firstborn with respect to their domestic cattle but 'redeemed' their firstborn children by means of an alternative animal sacrifice, and by treating circumcision as a kind of symbolic sacrifice of male children. The model for the first of these alternatives is provided by the story of Abraham's non-sacrifice of Isaac[111] and for the second by the story of Zipporah's circumcision of Moses' son Gershom,[112] cross-referenced to the circumcision of Isaac[113] and the assertion[114] that circumcision is a maker of God's covenant with Abraham. The story of Gershom's circumcision immediately follows a predictive reference to the slaying by God of the firstborn sons of the Egyptians.[115]

The relevance of all this to my main theme is as follows. The story of Moses in the Bulrushes and the story of the Nativity of the child Jesus are both linked with stories of the massacre of children by royal command.[116] They are not stories about sinful birth but about sinless rebirth; the purity of the infants concerned is established by the mass sacrifice of other children. The purified infants are replacements. The child that is discovered by the Princess and the child that is discovered by the Magi at Bethlehem are both children returned from the dead.

Hence the Dura representation of the ark of bulrushes as a coffin[117] and the lifting of the faceless child from the waters by an Ashtaroth mother-goddess.

With that background it should not surprise us that when, in the New Testament, Lazarus and Jesus both explicitly return from the dead they should emerge from caves (a very palpable womb symbol) and that their rebirth should be witnessed by women who are both the same and the precise opposite to the sinless Virgin of Christ's Nativity.

But the passage of time is also an element in this mythology. As a general rule mythological rebirth is simply a return to the beginning and this principle would apply to the present case if we were to accept, unqualified, the Frazerian view that the mythology of the mother-goddesses of the ancient world is a straightforward representation of the cycle of the seasons. But the Bible is not a farmer's calendar; it is a story about creation and perpetuation, first of the ancient Israelite nation and then of the 'New Israel', the Church of Christianity.

The theme of perpetuation is crucial. The continuity of society through death and rebirth entails replacement. Sons replace fathers; daughters replace mothers. But since the mother of the son was the bride of the son's father, the daughter of the mother must be bride to the son. That is the mytho-logic of the matter and it is explicit in the Osiris–Horus–Isis story. The biblical versions baulk at the more extreme incestuous implications but let us look once again at the essential details.

In the Moses story it is the mother who places the infant in the ark of bulrushes; she is witness to the death. It is the sister who observes the discovery of the infant by the Princess; she is witness to the rebirth. In the Christian story of the Crucifixion the mother of Jesus appears only once;

she is witness to the death. It is Mary Magdalene who is consistently the witness to the rebirth.

Why Mary Magdalene? She has sexual associations; she is a repentant sinner; a woman cleansed by Christ of contamination; a bearer of aphrodisiac ointments; in the Gnostic texts the lover of Christ in a erotic sense. She is not the mother of human children yet she is repeatedly linked with 'Mary, the Mother of James', the human successor to Jesus as head of the Church. But none of the texts suggest that Mary Magdalene is sister to Jesus.

For that matter the Old Testament Miriam is never described as the sister of Moses. Where named she is the prophetess, the 'sister of Aaron'.

But why a prophetess? In her prophetess role Miriam sings a song of triumph which clearly associates her with Deborah, the war leader of Judges 4–5 who is also a prophetess – i.e. a woman liable to be possessed by the Deity. It is also in her prophetess role that in Numbers 12 Miriam is stricken with leprosy. The purging by Moses of this symptom of malign possession corresponds to the casting out of seven devils from Mary Magdalene by Jesus.[118]

The leprosy from which Miriam is freed is specifically associated both with death and with birth:

> Let her not be as one dead, of whom the flesh is half consumed when he cometh out of his mother's womb[119]

The circumstances of this tale re-echo that of Abraham. Miriam the sister of Moses is jealous because he has taken an Ethiopian woman as wife; earlier Sarah, who was Abraham's half-sister as well as his wife, was jealous because his firstborn child had been born of an Egyptian woman, Hagar.[120] The text never suggests that Miriam is Moses' wife as well as his sister. Yet that is the logic of the total mythical construct: Miriam is Ashtoreth, the angel of death, lover and mother of the second birth, and that too is where Mary Magdalene fits into the Christian story.

Many years ago J. M. Robertson, a learned rationalist would-be debunker of Christianity, using a quite different, essentially Frazerian, methodology, arrived at precisely the same conclusion[121]. His main thesis was that the Jesus (Joshua) of the New Testament was a recapitulation of the Joshua of the Old Testament but, in the course of his researches, he discovered a Persian chronicle of antiquity which described Joshua as the son of Miriam. Elaborating on this he claimed, without any obvious justification, that 'Joshua was originally a variant of Tammuz and Miriam a variant of Ishtar.'[122] The convergence between Robertson's findings and my own does not mean that either of us is right, but since our methods are altogether different it is of some interest.

So what is the answer to my title question? Why did Moses have a sister? I would put it this way. The editing of the Bible texts into the canonical form which we now possess was a long-term process which began, in the case of the Old Testament, around the third Century B.C., but continued for many centuries. The attempts on the part of both Jewish and Christian editors to eliminate all traces of earlier 'heretical' opinion were only partially effective. Miriam in the Old Testament and Mary Magdalene in the New Testament reflect strains of religious thinking in which the idea that deity might be partly female was relatively acceptable.[123]

Which brings us back to the beginning. If Ashtaroth seems to belong to a world with which we have lost all contact, Kali is only a few hours away by Air India. In antiquity, as in modern India, the timeless, permanent aspects of deity were perceived as male, the ongoing, time-bound, creative/destructive aspect of deity as female. Orthodox Judaism and orthodox Christianity both endeavoured to eliminate the female element, but they succeeded in doing so only in a very formal sense. The canonical texts of the Bible retain large numbers of female characters who are mothers, sisters, wives, lovers, daughters to the male protagonists of the story who are, more obviously, semi-divine heroes of a standard type. These females have inevitably taken on the attributes of the goddesses of other religious systems. Some of these attributes have been discussed in the course of this essay.

Of all the Jewish patriarchs the one who comes closest to having the attributes of God incarnate is Moses.[124] Like the Jesus of Christianity he is both King and Prophet. All the paradoxes arise from that ambiguity. Divine Kings need to come from a lineage of Kings and their lineage must endure for ever. And that is precisely how the books of Exodus and Matthew start off ... with a genealogy; from Jacob through Levi to Moses in the first case,[125] from Abraham through David and Solomon and a line of Kings to 'Joseph the husband of Mary of whom was born Jesus, who is called Christ' in the second.[126] But ascetic Prophets of the Wilderness can only be heirs of the spirit, never heirs of the flesh. So Joshua follows Moses and Jesus follows John by a person to person transmission of Grace which is wholly independent of the contamination of sexuality and birth from the womb.

The extreme ambiguity of the female characters with whom these two 'sons of God' are associated derives from this contradiction; mytho-logic requires that the divine king-prophet shall be both married and unmarried, fertile and infertile, born of woman but not begotten of man.

I have tried to exhibit some of the ways in which biblical mythology seeks to resolve these puzzles but, as I have indicated by my reference to the Dura murals, I find that artists make a much better job of it than theologians.

Plate 4 shows a picture by Gaddi[127] which is in the National Gallery in Washington. Christ is crowning his mother as Queen of Heaven. Apart from the fact that Christ is already wearing his crown and the Madonna is not, the two figures are represented as virtually identical; they might well be twins.

A similar convention is to be found in many examples of Renaissance and medieval art. One such example is certainly known to you all. [See Plates 5 & 6].

Michelangelo's Pietà in Saint Peter's in Rome shows a young Madonna holding the dead body of her full grown son. This much you all know. The fact that the Madonna is so young was Michelangelo's choice.[128] So also was the fact that, as you probably do not know, he chose to give Christ and his mother almost identical features.[129]

Moses has a sister because mytho-logic requires that his mother should be no older than himself.

Notes

1 Brabrook (1896): 386–9.
2 Frazer (1918): I, 104–74.
3 The complexities of the metaphors of divine sexuality as they are worked out in Hindu theology are illustrated by O'Flaherty (1980) and Shulman (1980).
4 Two particularly readable accounts of the ambiguous roles of the Virgin Mary in Catholic theology are provided by Hirn (1912) and Warner (1976). There are mediaeval Carols which actually refer to her as a 'goddess'.
5 Ganesha, who is, *par excellence*, the mediator son of God in Saivite Hinduism, is likewise markedly effeminate.
6 Pagels (1979).
7 See Gutmann (1973) which includes a select bibliography of materials concerning the Dura synagogue. Of particular importance is Goodenough (1964): Vols. 9–11 from whom my illustrations [Figs. 4, 5, 6] and my interpretation of Fig. 5 are derived.

   Goodenough assumed that the presence of 'pagan' images in this provincial synagogue must be due to the existence in Dura of an unorthodox 'mystic' form of Judaism. But subsequent excavations in Palestine itself have demonstrated that comparable 'pagan' imagery was in use at this period even in the geographical heartland of Judaism. See Avi-Yonah (1973).

The other really major authority on the Dura synagogue murals is Kraeling (1956). Goodenough and Kraeling are in radical disagreement on many issues but on the particular problems of interpretation which I mention here Goodenough seems to have much the stronger case.

8 My position is thus fundamentally different from that of Pitt-Rivers (1977) which uses some of the same material in an essay designed as a critique of an earlier essay of my own. For Pitt-Rivers the 'ethnographic present' of the books of the Bible progresses chronologically; the Bible is a history book first and a sacred table second; the marital and sexual eccentricities of the patriarchs are to be explained by the fact that they lived at a time when the rules as spelled out in Leviticus and Deuteronomy had not yet been formulated.

Pitt-Rivers, who sees himself as a defender of Lévi-Straussian orthodoxy against Leachian heresy, summarises his argument as follows:

The book of Genesis appears to me to be the product of quite a different process from those pure myths that are found in illiterate unstratified societies who have no sense of the historical past and even from those which can be sensed rather than perceived *behind* the text of the early chapters of Genesis. Rather than stories each of a piece, complete in itself and related to other such stories by no established order, those of the Old Testament are diachronically ranged, even if the order differs slightly in the different versions (Torah, Vulgate, etc.), and rather than the unreasoned product of the collective consciousness, they are the consciously reasoned constructs of individual men attempting to find in the debris of events a pervasive sense, and looking to the past for an authority to be exercised in the present (*op. cit.*: 169).

In comment, I would reply that I myself have no use for the Durkheimian concept of a 'collective consciousness' (or for the more Lévi-Straussian concept of a 'collective unconsciousness'). Further, the notion of 'pure myths', in the sense used by Pitt-Rivers, is an invention of Lévi-Strauss which does not correspond to the experience of competent ethnographers. It is true that when myths are properly recorded in the field they are not always given in precisely the same order but they are always presented as a *corpus* which begins at the beginning with the creation of the world and continues down to the present. Lévi-Strauss' distinction between 'cold societies' (without history) and 'hot societies' (which exist within history), which Pitt-Rivers relies upon for his model (see note 86 at p. 186 of the cited reference) is one which I myself totally reject.

9 However, in the case of the New Testament, the heretical texts discussed by Pagels do provide us with direct evidence of some of the material that was rejected, while, for both the Old and the New Testaments, there exist a large number of Apocryphal writings which have, at different times, been accepted as 'more or less' canonical. The theme of my present essay is that the canonical texts as we *now* have them still contain traces of repeated editorial revision. In the texts which were rejected the Miriam (Mary) characters of both the Old and the New Testaments played a different, and probably more prominent, role from that which they fill in the modern canon.

10 1611 'King James Version' of the English Bible.

11 Numbers 12.1–8.

12 Numbers 20.23–9; 25.6–13.

13 Exodus 33.11; Numbers 11.28; Deuteronomy 34.9.

14 2 Kings 2.
15 Matthew 14.2; Mark 6.14, 16; Luke 9.7.
16 Note how in Numbers 11 and 12 the Tabernacle is presumed to be located outside the camp while God meets with Moses, Aaron and Miriam by standing on a further threshold 'in the door of the Tabernacle'. At Numbers 11. 26–8 the point is explicitly made that it is anomalous for anyone to prophesy within the camp.
17 Exodus 7:1. The parallels between Moses and Christ which impressed Freud (Freud (1939): 58ff.; 143ff.) are hardly justified by the biblical texts but the 'special relationship' between God and Moses is comparable to that which, in Islam, gives Mahomet a unique position as spokesman of God. Since Judaism and Islam have not qualified the central dogma of Monotheism by any equivocation analogous to the Christian Trinity, it is heresy to say that either Moses or Mahomet is 'a god', but they are certainly not ordinary human beings. Likewise, although tradition does not claim that they were 'kings' in a formal sense, they are nevertheless remembered as political rulers as well as prophets.
18 Matthew 3.3–4; 11.7–8; Genesis 41. 42f.; 1 Kings 11.1–4; Ezekiel 16. In this last reference God himself is represented as a King while 'Jerusalem' (Israel) is his lavishly adorned but faithless Queen.
19 Exodus 3.1.
20 Ezekiel 43.3–9.
21 1 Samuel 9.6–27; 10.1.
22 1 Samuel 10.5, 10–13.
23 1 Samuel 16.4, 12–13; 2 Samuel 2.1–4.
24 1 Samuel 16.11.
25 Matthew 2.1–2.
26 Matthew 3.1, 13.
27 Matthew 4.1–11.
28 Matthew 14.15–33.
29 Matthew 15.32–38; 17.1–9.
30 Matthew 21.1–15.
31 Anglican Book of Common Prayer: Morning Prayer: A prayer for the King's Majesty.
32 Luke 16.22–31.
33 Hooke (1933); Hooke (1935); Hocart (1927); Hocart (1936). See also discussion in Chapter 2 of this book.
34 Hocart (1927), Hocart (1936), Raglan (1936).
35 What matters here is repute. Practice was less straightforward. The human Egyptian Pharaohs did sometimes marry their full sisters, but so also did ordinary Egyptians (Hopkins (1980)), so we need to distinguish between myth and history. Unfortunately Egyptologists disagree among themselves as to the historical facts. Moreover most Egyptologists are anthropologically naive, introducing improbable references to residual matriarchy on the slightest provocation.
    The pattern of close-kin marriages in remote antiquity is unclear, but it is certain that at the beginning of the 18th Dynasty (approx. 1570–1546 B.C.) the Pharaoh Ahmose married his full sister Nofretari and that after her death Nofretari was worshipped as a goddess. Furthermore, at about this time, the eldest daughter of the Pharaoh's principal wife acquired the title

'God's wife' during childhood. The succeeding Pharaoh, whether or not he was the son of the previous Pharaoh, seems to have married the 'God's wife'. Thus Thutmose I married the 'God's wife' daughter of his predecessor Amonhotep. Thutmose II married the daughter of this union, Hatshepsut, who was his half-sister. Thutmose III was the son of Thutmose II by a junior wife and thus a legitimate heir but, while he was a minor, his stepmother Hatshepsut appears to have ruled, not simply as a regent but with the full rank of Pharaoh, apparently because she was a 'God's wife'.

In succeeding dynasties the custom of close-kin marriages within the royal family seems to have been less important but it was actively revived during the Hellenistic Ptolemaic dynasty, 330–30 B.C. In particular, Ptolemy II was married to his full sister Arsinoe II and in the period 284–270 B.C. they were recognised as joint rulers. Arsinoe was worshipped as a goddess after her death. The pattern here exactly replicates the model provided by Ahmose and Nofretari 1300 years earlier. This Ptolemaic revival of the brother–sister marriage-pattern is relevant to my theme since it would have provided the editors of biblical texts working at that period with a confirmatory exemplar of what was believed to be traditional Pharaonic behaviour. For details of the 'God's wife' title see Sander-Hansen (1940).

In contradiction to what is here implied Frankfort (1948) [44ff., 73ff., 181–5] claimed that although the living Pharaoh, in his status as Horus, was 'son of Isis' there is little evidence that divinity was attributed to the human mother of the reigning Pharaoh. On that account he argued that Isis was not so much a personification of the human queen as a personification of a more abstract entity 'the throne'. I am not personally persuaded that the Egyptians thought about matters in this way, though such a formula may help to make the dogmas of positional succession more easily comprehensible to modern Europeans.

The surviving texts of the Osiris mythology (and related mythologies) are so incomplete as to allow for a variety of interpretations. From a structuralist point of view it is of interest that the only seemingly complete and coherent version of the story comes from a foreign source (Plutarch in 'On Isis and Osiris' in the *Moralia*).

For an application of the anthropologist's concept of 'positional succession' to the Egyptian material and a list of scholarly references see Leach (1976).

36 Genesis 20.12.
37 Personal communication from Dr Martin Bernal.
38 Genesis 12.10–20. Pitt-Rivers (1977): 151–6 discussess the same material which he uses in quite a different way to exemplify his thesis that the diachronic ordering of the stories exhibits historical progression in the development of moral ideas rather than the synchronic mode of myth. For Pitt-Rivers the story of Dinah (Genesis 34) is a crux. He argues that before this chapter a form of sexual hospitality was customary; after this chapter it was not. The stories of Sarah and Rebekah as sister-wife exhibit these princesses as women 'who might legitimately be given away to a powerful stranger', whereas the story of Dinah asserts that 'since Dinah is really sister and only sister, [...] women cannot be given away at all'. 'There is a progression therefore from the first [story] to the second, in the direction of restricting the access of foreigners to Israelite women.' Pitt-Rivers then goes

on to claim that this kind of 'progression' is generally characteristic of biblical stories which exhibit structural similarity (p. 156–8).

I offer detailed criticism of this last argument in Chapter 2 of this book, but I am also quite unimpressed by Pitt-Rivers arguments about wife-lending. It is true than an institution of wife-lending has been reported from many parts of the world, but there does not seem to be the slightest evidence that any such custom was anywhere prevalent in ancient times in any part of the Middle East. I agree that Dinah is introduced into the story in order that she shall suffer sexual dishonour and thereby become a pattern for the rule of endogamy among Israelite women. But Pitt-Rivers' polarisation of the story of Dinah (Genesis 34) to that of Sarah (Chapter 12) seems highly contrived. A more obvious polarisation would be with Genesis 31 where Laban allows Jacob to abduct his daughters because Jacob is a kinsman whereas, in Genesis 34, Hamor is not allowed to abduct the sister of Jacob's sons because he is not their kinsman.

39 cf. Genesis 12.4; 17.17.
40 Genesis 20.
41 Genesis 26.6–16.
42 Hastings (1909): 4.
43 Genesis 12.10.
44 Matthew 2.13–14.
45 Exodus 14.21–8; Joshua, Chs 3 and 4.
46 Turner (1969).
47 Genesis 39.7–10.
48 Genesis 41.40–5.
49 Hastings (1909): 740–1. This is a distortion of a genuine Egyptian name: 'Petepre' – 'given by Re (the Sun-God)'.
50 Genesis 46.20. The name Asenath is a genuine Egyptian name meaning 'dedicated to Neit'. Neit was the patron goddess of the 26th Dynasty. This implies that the original story is later than the 7th Century B.C. (cf. Hastings (1909) : 55).
51 Genesis 41.42–43.
52 1 Chronicles 23.1.
53 1 Kings 3.2.
54 2 Samuel 11.
55 Josephus *The Antiquities of the Jews* VIII: vi: 5f.
56 1 Kings 1.2–4.
57 1 Kings 2.17–25.
58 Exodus 6.20.
59 Leviticus 20.19.
60 Exodus 2.3–10.
61 Exodus 2.1–2.
62 For references to sources see Clark (1959): 186ff.
63 Matthew 2.16; Exodus 1.16.
64 The 'wise men' of Matthew 2.1 are nowhere said to be three in number and they are nowhere described as kings. It is Luke 2.7 who has the story of the babe laid in a manger and he makes the shepherds his witnesses to the birth. Matthew's wise men find the child 'in the house' (Matthew 2.11).

65 For summary and references see Clark (1959): 195–208; also Leach (1976).
66 Exodus 2.15–3.6.
67 Numbers 12.1.
68 Genesis 21.2; 25.21–3; 30.22–4; 38.1–30; Ruth *passim*; 2 Samuel 11.2–27; 12.15–25; Matthew 1.18–25.
69 Genesis 34.
70 2 Samuel 13.1–33.
71 Judges 4.4–5.41.
72 1 Kings 16.31; 18.19–19.3; 21.1–25.
73 Micah 6.4.
74 Numbers 19.11–22. The only other mention of a Miriam in the Old Testament comes in a garbled text at 1 Chronicles 4.17. This Miriam is apparently male. It is however interesting that, if the editorial adjustments to the text used in the New English Bible are accepted, then this Miriam is the child of a daughter of Pharaoh. The name seems to mean 'beloved of Amon'.
75 Warner (1976) Ch. 15, 'The Penitent Whore', has some very pertinent remarks on the complementary roles of Mary the unsullied mother and Mary the sullied but repentant sinner, e.g.:

Together the Virgin and the Magdalene form a diptych of Christian patriarchy's ideas of woman. There is no place in the conceptual architecture of Christian society for a single woman who is neither a virgin nor a whore.

76 John 11.5. 'Now Jesus loved Martha, and her sister, and Lazarus.' This is not said of any of the other followers of Jesus except of 'the disciple whom Jesus loved', who was traditionally identified both with St John the Apostle, son of Zebedee and brother to James, and St John the Evangelist supposed author of both St John's gospel and the Book of Revelation. The 'special relationship' which is thus implied seems to be introduced in order to justify the exceptional treatment of Lazarus who is raised from the dead (John 11.1–46). But this makes Lazarus a kind of *alter* of Jesus himself.
77 I rely here on Pagels' summaries of the Nag Hammadi texts (see especially Pagels [1979]: pp. 18, 49, 64, 65). But see also Warner (1976), references at pp. 229, 382; in particular Phipps (1970), which is a serious work.
78 John 11.32–45.
79 As Graces the visitors bear gifts; as Nymphs they may have the role of nurses. For a very full discussion with extensive scholarly references see Goodenough (1964) Vol. 9: 203–24.
80 For discussion see Goodenough Ch. 9. The principal difference between this drawing and the restored original now in Damascus is that, in the restoration, the baby who is being lifted out of the water has been given a face. Kraeling explains the facelessness of the infants concerned as due to vandalism in antiquity.
81 See Goodenough 9.198–9 who is here supported by other experts.
82 See Goodenough 9.200.ff. for full discussion.
83 Goodenough Vol. 9 p. 198 discussess an illustration (Vol. 11.175) in the twelfth Century Constantinople Octateuch, which shows the Moses birth-story in two scenes. In the upper half the Princess, accompanied by a

servant, discovers the baby in a box while Miriam hides behind some trees; in the lower half the Princess accompanied by two women (presumably Jochabed and Miriam) presents Moses who is already a grown boy to Pharaoh on his throne. Pharaoh, the Princess, and Moses all have haloes, indicating their para-divine status.

84 Coffin Texts IV, 147 quoted by Clark (1959): 88.
85 Clark (1959): 101.
86 Ezekiel 16, 23; Hosea Chs 1–9.
87 Canticles 3.6; 4.6. For the aphrodisiac associations of frankincense and myrrh in Ancient Greece see Detienne (1972), Detienne (1977).
88 Matthew 2.11.
89 Warner (1976): Chapter 8.
90 New English Bible (1970): footnote to Luke 24.10.
91 Goodenough 1: Chapter 3 and 3: esp. Figures 32, 91.
92 Luke 8.3.
93 Mark 3.17; Luke 14.3–12.
94 Matthew 14.3–11; Mark 6.17–29. The most recent 'definitive' Vatican statement on these matters, while recognising the ambiguities, concludes that 'in all probability' [*con ogni probibilità*] Salome the mother of James and John, the sons of Zebedee, was the 'sister' of the Virgin Mary mentioned in John 19.25. But it also suggests that Salome's name is a corruption of 'Jacopi', her real name being Mary. (*Bibliotheca Sanctorum* (1968): Vol XI: Col. 583.). Another angle on this confusion of Marys is provided by the fact that one of the great pilgrimage-centres of the Middle Ages was the church of Les Saintes Maries in the Camargue. The two principal Marys in question are Mary, the mother of St James the Less and Mary Salome, the mother of the sons of Zebedee. A local myth tangles them up still further (see Mazel (1935)).
95 The ambiguities only arise because, possessing a standardised canon of written texts which Christians choose to treat as history, we try to make literal sense of all the conflicting stories simultaneously. When myth is transmitted wholly or mainly as an oral tradition (as must have been the case for at least the first two generations of early Christians), we do not expect to find consistency of detail between one story and another.
96 1 Corinthians 17.7; Galatians 1.18–19; Galatians 2.1–10; Acts 21.18–19.
97 Hastings (1909): 424.
98 Matthew 4.5; Luke 4.9.
99 Luke 1.7.
100 Luke 1.36.
101 In the sense that archaeology has revealed the existence of 'topheth' sites where the sacrifice of human children certainly took place.
102 Hastings (1909): 58.
103 In Hinduism 'the Goddess' (Devi) has different names according to her role. As the active force of Creation she is Parvati, as Preserver she is Durga, as Destroyer she is Kali ('the black one') and so on. If we put all the roles of Devi together she resembles very closely the Ashtaroth of the Ancient World.
104 2 Kings 23.
105 Frazer (1914): Vol. 4 Chapter VI.

106 Genesis 16.1–12; Genesis 21.1–17.
107 Genesis 27.1–41.
108 Genesis 38.27–30.
109 2 Samuel 12.
110 Leviticus 16.7–10. Hastings (1909) p. 77 article 'Azazel' makes much better anthropological sense than the New English Bible translation 'precipice'.
111 Genesis 22.
112 Exodus 4.24–6.
113 Genesis 21.4.
114 Genesis 17.9–14.
115 Exodus 4.23.
116 Exodus 1.16; Matthew 2.16.
117 The Septuagint *arca* (English biblical 'Ark' = chest) covers two distinct Hebrew words of which the one *tebhah* referred to both Noah's ark and to Moses' ark of bulrushes, while the other *'aron* covered the Ark of the Covenant, the Temple chest of 2 Kings 12.10 and Joseph's coffin (Genesis 50.26). In mediaeval Christian iconography Noah's ark quite frequently had the form of a coffin or sarcophagus.
118 Exodus 15.20.
119 Numbers 12.12.
120 Genesis 21.9–11.
121 Robertson (1928) 165–7: 396 ff. The first edition of this work appeared in 1911. Also relevant is Frazer (1914) Vol. 9 pp. 412 ff. Note on 'The Crucifixion of Christ'. Although the Book of Esther is a late text (? second century B.C.) the main characters in the story: Esther (Ishtar), Mordecai (Merodach, Marduk), Haman (Hamman), Vashti, all have the names of Babylonian and Elamite deities. The book purports to provide an origin myth for the Jewish Feast of Purim (which incidentally features prominently in the murals of the Dura-Europos synagogue). There is no manifest link between the biblical Esther and any of the biblical Miriams.
122 Robertson (1928) p. 166.
123 cf Pagels (1979) *passim*.
124 Moses is not of course formally represented as 'divine', but the passion with which Buber (1952) writes in defence of the orthodox view that Moses was a real, historical, fully human individual points to the strength of the contrary attitudes even within orthodox Judaism. Buber pours scorn on Freud's view of Moses, and this is no doubt partly deserved, yet Freud's view that the Old Testament represents Moses as the First Messiah whose eventual replacement will bring world redemption seems to me incontrovertible.
125 Exodus 1.1–7.
126 Matthew 1.1–17.
127 Agnoli Gaddi *Coronation of the Virgin*. Another iconographic device for emphasising the role of the Virgin as the Bride of Christ was to show the two figures facing one another and holding each other by the right hand in the nuptial gesture of *dextrarum junctio*. There is an example in the Museum of Fine Arts, Boston which is illustrated in Warner (1976), Figure 17.
128 The original image of the *Pietà* (Mary cradling the body of the dead Christ) was a German rather than an Italian invention. Michelangelo's *Pietà* now in St Peter's in Rome was commissioned by a French cardinal, Jean Villiers de

Fezenzac. There is evidence from Vasari that Michelangelo's Italian contemporaries assumed that Mary's unusual youthfulness was suggested by a passage in Dante's *Paradiso*:

Vergine Madre, figlia del tuo Figlio...

Virgin Mother, daughter of your Son...

(see Hibbard (1979): p. 28).

129 The details of the face of the dead Christ cannot be seen by the ordinary observer.

References

Avi-Yonah, M. 1973 'The Dura-Europos Synagogue: a Critique', in Gutmann (1973): 117–35

Bible 1970 *The New English Bible with the Apocrypha*, Oxford: Oxford University Press

Bibliotheca Sanctorum 1961–70 [1968] Rome, Instituto Giovanni XXIII della Pontificia Università Lateranense

Brabrook, E. W. 1896 'President's anniversary address: Section 12: "T. H. Huxley"; *Journal of the Anthropological Institute* Vol. 25:386–9

Buber, M. 1952 *Moses*, Heidelberg: Verlag Lambert Schneider

Clark, R. T. Rundle 1959 *Myth and Symbol in Ancient Egypt*, London: Thames and Hudson

Detienne, M. 1972 *Les Jardins d'Adonis: La Mythologie des aromates en Grece*, Paris: NRF-Gallimard

1977 *Dyonysos mis a mort*, Paris: NRF-Gallimard

Frankfort, H. 1948 *Kingship and the Gods: A Study of Ancient Near Eastern Religion as the Integration of Society and Nature*, Chicago: The University of Chicago Press

Frazer, J. G. 1911–15, 1936 *The Golden Bough*, 3rd Edition: 13 Volumes, London: Macmillan

1918 *Folklore in the Old Testament: Studies in Comparative Religion, Legend and Law*, 3 Vols. London: Macmillan

Freud, S. 1939 *Moses and Monotheism*, London: Hogarth Press and The Institute of Psycho Analysis

Goodenough, E. R. 1964 *Jewish Symbols in the Greco-Roman Period*: Vols 9–11: *Symbolism in the Dura Synagogue*, Bollingen Series XXXVII, New York: Pantheon Books

Gutmann, J. (Ed.) 1973 *The Dura-Europos Synagogue: A Re-evaluation (1932–1972)*, Missoula: University of Montana Printing Dept. [American Academy of Religion: Society of Biblical Literature]

Hastings, J. (Ed.) 1909 *Dictionary of the Bible*, Edinburgh: T. & T. Clark

Hibbard, H. 1975 *Michelangelo: Painter, Sculptor, Architect*, London: Allen Lane/Penguin Books Ltd

Hirn, Yrjo 1912 *The Sacred Shrine: A Study of the Poetry and Art of the Catholic Church*, London: Macmillan

Hocart, A. M. 1927 *Kingship*, London: Oxford University Press

1936 *Kings and Councillors: An Essay in the Comparative Anatomy of Human Society*, Cairo: Printing Office Paul Barbey

Hooke, S. H. (Ed.) 1933 *Myth and Ritual: Essays in the Myth and Ritual of the Hebrews in Relation to the Culture Pattern of the Near East*, London: Oxford University Press

(ed.) 1935 *The Labyrinth: Further Studies in the Relation between Myth and Ritual in the Ancient World*, London: S.P.C.K.

Hopkins, K. 1980 'Brother-Sister Marriage in Roman Egypt', *Comparative Studies in Society and History*, Vol. 22: No. 3 (July 1980): 303–54

Kraeling, C. H. 1956 *The Synagogue. The Excavations at Dura-Europos. Final Report* VIII, Part 1, New Haven: Yale University Press

Leach, E. 1969 *'Genesis as Myth' and Other Essays*, London: Jonathan Cape

1976 'The Mother's Brother in Ancient Egypt', in *R.A.I.N.* (Royal Anthropological Institute News) No. 15: (August 1976): 19–21

Mazel, A. 1935 *Les Saintes Maries de la Mer et la Camargue*, (Vaison-la-Romaine: Impr. Soc. de la Bonne Presse du Midi) [reprinted 1955]

O'Flaherty, W. D. 1980 *Women, Androgynes and Other Mythical Beasts*, Chicago: The University of Chicago Press

Pagels, Elaine 1979 *The Gnostic Gospels*, London: Weidenfeld and Nicolson

Phipps, W. 1970 *Was Jesus Married?: The Distortion of Sexuality in the Christian Tradition*, New York: Harper and Row

Pitt-Rivers, J. 1977 *The Fate of Shechem or the Politics of Sex: Essays in the Anthropology of the Mediterranean*, Cambridge Studies in Social Anthropology No. 19, Cambridge: Cambridge University Press

Raglan, Lord 1936 *The Hero: A Study in Tradition, Myth and Drama*, London: Methuen and Co.

Robertson, J. M. 1911 *Pagan Christs: Studies in Comparative Hierology* (2nd Edition), London: Watts and Co. for the Rationalist Press Association

Sander-Hansen, C. E. 1940 *Das Gottesweib des Amun* [Hist.-Filol. Skr. Udg. af. det. Kgl. Dansk Vidersnsk. Selsk., I (i)], Copenhagen

Shulman, D. D. 1980 *Tamil Temple Myths: Sacrifice and Divine Marriage in the South India Saiva Tradition*, Princeton, N. J.: Princeton University Press

Turner, V. W. 1969 *The Ritual Process: Structure and Anti-Structure*, London: Routledge and Kegan Paul

Warner, Marina 1976 *Alone of All Her Sex: The Myth and Cult of the Virgin Mary*, London: Weidenfeld and Nicolson

1   Three graces attend the birth of the virgin.

2 The Infancy of Moses as depicted in the Dura-Synagogue (3rd century A.D.)

3 Anahita.

4 The Coronation of the Virgin with Angels, Altar-piece

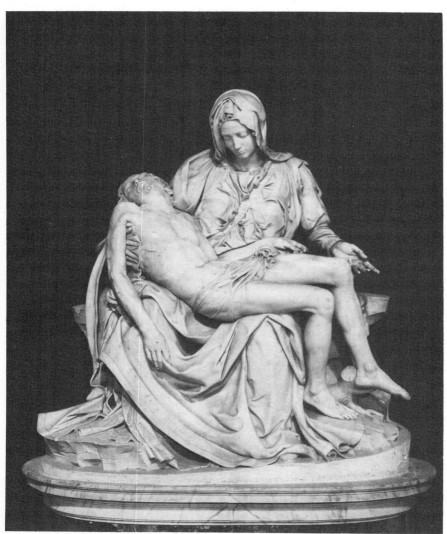

5 Michelangelo, Pietà, Vatican.

6 Close-up of two heads.

4 Melchisedech and the emperor: icons of subversion and orthodoxy*

EDMUND LEACH

I must start on a note of apology. In a well-intentioned attempt to design a lecture which would interest a wide variety of people I have landed myself with a topic which is far too large for its allotted space. You must forgive me if, in the interests of compression, I leave a large number of loose ends unexplained.

Consider first of all the diagram shown in Fig. 1. This schema represents a cosmological system in which impotent Man on Earth is polarised against omnipotent God in Heaven. Religion is concerned with mediation between the two spheres such that a channel is provided through which divine potency from Heaven is brought to bear upon the affairs of impotent Man on Earth.

Ethnography reveals a variety of possible mediating systems of this general type but two particular patterns are especially frequent. The first is that of *sacrifice*. The mediator is a human being, the priest of the sacrifice, who acts on behalf of a lay congregation. The sacrificial rite is viewed as an 'offering' to the Deity, and the priest, who stands in a superior position *vis-à-vis* his congregation, is in a suppliant status *vis-à-vis* the Deity.

In my title I refer to this hierarchical model as 'an icon of orthodoxy'. Later in the lecture I shall show how it is given visual expression in certain Ravenna mosaics made in the time of the Emperor Justinian with the express purpose of asserting the emperor's identification with orthodox catholic theology.

In the second pattern it is God who takes the initiative by offering grace to the faithful. The individual devotee is directly inspired. The charisma is a direct gift from God which is in no way dependent upon the ritual efficacy of a mediating human priest. This non-hierarchical model is what I describe as 'an icon of subversion'. In empirical circumstances it is closely associated with millenarian belief and heretical radicalism. This model also finds expression in early Christian art.

The next topic that I would have you consider is the general theory of millenarian cults as discussed in the recent writings of historians and social

*Presidential Address 1972

anthropologists (e.g. Cohn 1957; 1962; Worsley 1957; Hobsbawm 1959; Thrupp 1962). The authors concerned have repeatedly observed that in practically every well-documented case the basic chiliastic doctrine has its roots in ideas that were current among Judaeo-Christians of the first century A.D. The cargo cults of Melanesia, the Ghost Dance of the North American Indians, and the Taiping rebels of nineteenth-century China were all equally, in their devious fashion, derivations from the Biblical Book of Revelation. Yet I know of no study which has attempted to apply modern millenarian theory to the known facts of early Christianity. One of my objectives this evening is to suggest that there are some problems in this area which deserve much closer attention. One of these problems is the age-old topic of the Arian heresy.

A standard manual (Kelly 1958: 232) of early Christian doctrine roundly declares that:

> we have little or no first hand evidence of the reasons animating the fathers of Nicaea in their repudiation of Arianism.

I shall propose a piece of second-hand sociological evidence on this topic which seems to have been largely neglected.

My starting point, which is based on much wider reading than some of you may care to give me credit for, is the following. The origin of Christianity lay in a wide-ranging cultural situation rather than in any single event. From as early as the second century B.C., the jumble of Egyptian, Hellenistic, Jewish and Persian ideologies that were current in the eastern Mediterranean area had provided the eschatology for a whole series of millenarian cults that were so closely related to one another that to a contemporary outsider they appeared indistinguishable. Present-day Christian commentators describe Gnosticism as 'the product of syncretism which drew upon Jewish pagan and oriental sources of inspiration'.[1] I myself consider that the same is true of Christianity itself. There was not just one primitive Christian church; there were many.

But if first-century Christianity consisted of a collectivity of overlapping millenarian sects rather than a unitary church, then, from a comparative point of view, the history of the Puritan sects in seventeenth-century England becomes directly relevant. And with Max Weber in the background, *that* kind of cross-reference must immediately lead any social anthropologist to ask: in what sense was early Christian doctrine intermeshed with its social context?

It is astonishing to find how little attention has been paid to this rather obvious problem. Although the experts give full prominence to the way in which political intrigue influenced the outcome of individual

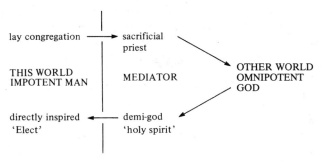

Figure 1. Sacrifice and inspiration: alternative cosmological schema.

Church Synods and Councils they have shown little interest in the social background of belief as such.

As a result, the seemingly endless debate about the nature of the Trinity and the limits of Christ's humanity continues to be treated as if it were part of an ongoing seminar continued over centuries within the closed doors of a University Faculty of Theology. Even the most recent textbooks still manage to convey the impression that the early Christian Church was a scholastic madhouse wholly preoccupied with subtleties of verbal definition.

The counter-argument which I am about to present to you, however defective it may be from the point of view of scholarship, at least makes sociological sense. At long last I begin to feel that I understand what the Arian controversy was all about.

During my professional life-time, social anthropologists have discussed the sociology of religion in two very different ways.

At the outset, when functionalism of the Malinowskian sort was in its heyday, it was taken for granted that religion, like everything else, was a conservative force contributing to the internal balance of the self-perpetuating social order. Even as late as 1959, Raymond Firth (1964:246) declared that 'religion helps to maintain, to support the social values upon which the continuance of the society depends', though he went on to admit that 'religion does not always perform these stated social functions'. Historians of radical inclination were particularly staunch in their defence of this position. In line with Marx's dictum that 'Religion is the opium of the people' they took it to be self-evident that organised religion is not only conservative but a part of the apparatus of oppression manipulated by the ruling class.[2]

But during the last few years the change of emphasis has been quite dramatic. Triggered off, it would seem, by the historical sophistication of Norman Cohn's wide-ranging studies of millenarianism in medieval Europe and Peter Worsley's oversimplified Marxist interpretation of Melanesian cargo cults (Cohn 1957; 1962; Worsley 1957), left-wing English historians have really gone to town on the protestant cults of the early seventeenth century. As a result, the religion of the Levellers, the Diggers, the Seekers, the Ranters, the Fifth Monarchy Men, the Quakers, the Muggletonians and the rest of Christopher Hill's merry crew is now displayed to us as a force of revolutionary liberation (Hill 1972).

As you will appreciate, these two models of the function of religious belief correspond to my twin icons of orthodoxy and subversion but they are not necessarily mutually exclusive or contradictory. At different times, in different places, Emperor and Anarchist alike may find it convenient to appeal to Holy Writ.

But the shift of register from innovation to conservatism and back to innovation again is a complex process which calls for detailed analysis.

If there are genuine regularities about these social oscillations, the decipherment of such 'process' certainly falls within the province of social anthropology, but, since the data that must be called in evidence need to be historical and spread over a considerable period of years, the social anthropologist, on his own account, is ill-equipped to do anything about it. In order to formulate a hypothesis of dialectical development he must borrow materials from other people. That is the justification for my present procedure.

So far as the analysis of millenarianism in seventeenth-century England is concerned the historians are now fully engaged. The social anthropologists have nothing more to do except stand on the side-lines and profit from the ensuing combat. In what has been published so far, two points seem particularly relevant to my problem.

First, it is evident that even in this highly literate seventeenth-century society, myth could readily dominate over historical fact. For example, long before 1659 it was being widely noised abroad, and seemingly believed by 'sober and eminent persons' that it was the Jesuits who had executed the King in 1649 (Lamont 1972: 79). In the light of my field-work experience as a social anthropologist this does not really surprise me, but it must be disconcerting for theologians who would like to persuade themselves that the Synoptic Gospels are a repository of historical truth. The plain implications of the English material is that when a spirit of heresy-hunting is around, even the most 'sensible' people are liable to believe almost anything. Any connection between historical fact and belief becomes purely accidental.

The second point of significance is the way that the seventeenth-century sects were mixed up, not only over issues of doctrine, but in their personnel. In the course of a few years a single individual might move right across the doctrinal and political spectrum. As Lamont puts it (1972:88): 'The young Milton looked for the establishment of a New Jerusalem in five weeks; the mature Milton extolled the patience of Job.'

We find the same pattern among the Christian Fathers of the second century. There was no generally accepted orthodoxy; tolerance and heresy-hunting went hand in hand. 'I and many others' says Justin Martyr (1861: Ch. 79) 'believe that the millennium will come to pass ... but there are at the same time many of a pure and devout Christian mind who are not of the same opinion; however, as for those who are called Christians, but are in reality godless and impious heretics, I have already proved that they teach all that is blasphemous, and atheistical and foolish.'

Such parallels are surely significant. Christianity in its earliest phase was a millenarian movement in the literal sense of that term. If some things are true about millenarian movements as a class they should be true of primitive Christianity.

But *what* is true about millenarian movements as a class? Those who are familiar with the very extensive literature on this topic (cf. Thrupp 1962; Lanternari 1963) will know how difficult it is to give a clear-cut answer. All that I would want to argue is that the following characteristics, which are found in early Christianity, appear also in a great number of other millenarian cults both ancient and modern.

First, the millenarian tradition is not simply a theory about the approach of the Last Judgement; it is a theory about temporal recapitulation. The sacred record of what has happened in the past can be turned back to front and used as a sacred prediction of what is going to happen in the future.

Secondly, anxious concern with the end of time tends to reach a maximum in periods of exceptional political uncertainty. At such times the devout sectarian's anxiety to be found among the Elect on the Day of Judgement goes along with an obsessional concern with the pursuit of heretics.

Thirdly, it is a necessary precondition for the formation of a *new* millenarian movement that the secular context from which it emerges should *already* contain, in embryo, a self-identifiable community which can readily be led to perceive itself as alienated from the interests of the paramount political power. There are many possible sources for this initial alienation – colonial conquest, the rise of a new economic class, survival from some natural disaster, persecution of an ethnic minority – but the end result is the same. Millenarianism is a creed for those who *feel* themselves to be deprived; it arises as a movement of protest against

71

rulers who claim to exercise authority by divine right rather than as representatives of the General Will.

The adherents of a new cult are not necessarily impoverished; some may be relatively wealthy. Indeed the missionary-apostles of the movement must always be persons of education and sophistication. But those who join a *new* cult always feel themselves to be *politically* under-privileged; in a political sense, they come from the bottom of the heap.[3] They are people who are excluded from all positions of real authority by the conventions of the existing system.

In this initial phase, the political theory of millenarian sects is always markedly egalitarian, with either communist or anarchist leanings. It is also markedly impractical. But although millenarian prophets are inclined to attack the existing social system with words rather than deeds, they almost invariably come to be regarded as a threat to the legitimate forces of law and order. The persecution and martyrdom which is a standard part of the syndrome is an automatic consequence of this situation.

However, as time goes on, individual members of the persecuted anarchist minority begin to acquire social and political respectability. At this stage millenarian doctrines fade into the background. In the long run the heirs to the preachers of heresy are likely to end up as the mouth-pieces of an established orthodoxy upon which the political regime leans for support.

That formula is extremely general but there are plenty of concrete examples. The evolution of English Quakerism since 1651 provides a copy-book example.

In its beginnings, the Quaker movement was on the extreme left. Its members were closely associated with the recklessly anarchist Ranters. Millenarianism was carried so far that in 1656 James Nayler claimed to be Christ incarnate and rode into Bristol mounted on an ass to symbolise His Second Coming. Both he and George Fox, the other founding Quaker preacher, were repeatedly imprisoned and the whole sect suf-fered vigorous political persecution and exclusion from office for over thirty years. Yet by 1800 the leading Quaker families were already wealthy and influential and have subsequently acquired an outstanding reputation for political good sense and social responsibility.

This overall process is what Max Weber described as 'the routinisation of charisma' (1947: 334f.).

The comparable evidence for the early Christian case is patchy but significant. The document known as the *Didache*, the relevant portions of which belong to the latter part of the first century (see Richardson 1953: 161–82), presupposes a world into which James Nayler and

George Fox would have fitted perfectly. The Church had no central organisation, no temples, no altars. The local sectarian communities were visited by itinerant 'God inspired'[4] prophets, but they also employed their own 'bishop' who was an ordained minister. The latter had assistants of either sex, known as 'deacons'. There was no large-scale hierarchy of church officials though as early as the end of the first century the Bishop of Rome was already claiming that he was uniquely qualified to decide issues of doctrine because of his direct apostolic succession from Peter and Paul (Clement: Chs. 42–4, in Richardson 1953).

One common heritage of the rival Christian sects was the belief that they were the new Israelites; the new Chosen People. The Jewish scriptures were interpreted as prefigurations of the Christian revelation. Christ is a second Adam; Moses leading the Israelites across the Red Sea pursued by the armies of Pharaoh is separating the Elect from the Damned. Incidentally a much later, fourth-century, pictorial representation of this scene shows the Elect austerely dressed as respectable Roman citizens while the Damned are a military rabble wearing Phrygian (i.e. Mithraic) hats![5]

Early second-century texts indicate that the faithful mostly imagined that they were living close to the end of time. A physical millennium on this earth was close at hand. Jerusalem was to be rebuilt and inhabited for 1000 years by the resurrected Elect (Dodgson 1854: 123).

It is notable that in the *Didache* (Chs. 9; 10; 14.2; Clement 44.4, in Richardson 1953) the sacrament of the Eucharist is viewed primarily as a common sacred meal through which the communicants assimilate to themselves the physical body of Christ as mediator. Although the rite is described as a sacrifice (*thusia*), the doctrine of universal redemption is missing. Jesus is a secondary being described as the servant (? child) of God. The pattern is that of the lower part of my Fig. 1 rather than that of the top.

In subsequent centuries there was a dialectical development corresponding to the success or failure of particular prelates in Rome or Constantinople or Alexandria or Antioch to assert paramountcy over ecclesiastical sees of varying scale. Wherever ecclesiastical hierarchy became elaborated millenarian doctrine fell into disfavour; *vice versa*, wherever a local schismatic church reasserted its independence millenarian belief once again became prominent.[6]

Such changes depended upon changes in interpretation rather than alteration of the scriptures. Thus Irenaeus (second century) declares explicitly that there is nothing allegorical about the imminent resurrection of the dead (cf. Dodgson 1854: 120 ff.), but by A.D. 230 Origen was already representing the New Jerusalem as belonging to the order of

Platonic ideas rather than of earthly facts (cf. Kelly 1958: 472–3). By the fifth century Christianity had become the official State religion, so implicitly revolutionary doctrines were quite out of place. St Augustine, who died in A.D. 430, spent the last years of his life teaming up with the political authorities in their forcible suppression of the separatist and millenarian adherents of the Donatist heresy in north Africa. Although, in his youth, Augustine had himself inclined towards millenarian belief he now declared that the Millennium was simply a symbol standing for the entire Christian era.[7]

Throughout these centuries of doctrinal oscillation and evolution, the formulae of belief propounded by those who anticipated an imminent physical millennium here on earth were invariably 'Arian in style'.

I must try to explain what I mean by that anachronistic statement.

Properly speaking, the particular doctrinal controversy known to history as the Arian heresy originated in A.D. 318 in Alexandria in a local quarrel between the Bishop and his Presbyter and was settled once and for all by the Council of Nicaea seven years later. But the issues that lay in that background of the quarrel had already been a source of worry for generations and several centuries were to elapse before the Nicene ruling became completely accepted by the whole Christian Church. Indeed, in diverse forms, the controversy has persisted right down to the present day. The radically millenarian Jehovah's Witnesses are avowed followers of Arius.

Modern orthodoxy in all the established Churches, both in the East and in the West, accepts the Nicene ruling and is thus both dyophysite and anti-Arian, but most of those who are now considered to be representative early Christian Fathers of the second and third centuries originally expressed themselves in Arian style.

This is an essential point in my argument. The early Christian sects were both millenarian and Arian in disposition and the two characteristics are closely associated. The denunciation of Arianism in A.D. 325 was part and parcel of the decay of millenarian doctrine which followed logically from the political emancipation of the Church at large.

The precise point at issue is not easily expounded. The rival theorists were attempting to derive diametrically opposite implications from the same passages of Holy Writ and they hurled abuse at one another very much in the contemporary style of high-ranking officials of Moscow and Peking. In the literature of the fourth century the label 'Arian' is often no more illuminating than is 'Marxist-Leninist-Bourgeois-Deviationist', but if you go back to the second century and follow the argument through to the sixth you will find that there is an evolution. Although the same themes constantly recur, there is a gradual shift of emphasis: the authority of ordained priests replaces the revelation of inspired prophets; the Crucifixion supplants the Incarnation as the doctrinal crux.

In the earliest texts it is the *birth* of the Christ–Logos as second Adam which brings enlightenment to the Elect and which marks the beginning of New Time; only later does the emphasis come to fall on the Crucifixion as the redemptive sacrifice for all mankind. In earlier versions the Millennium is to *precede* the Last Judgement, implying that the Elect are already known; later the sequence is reversed, the Millennium is a reward for the virtuous in the last days which are still far off.[8]

All such changes imply a shift away from my 'icon of subversion' towards my 'icon of orthodoxy', but mostly they lie in the background. In a more formal sense the main worry was over the nature of Deity and the humanity of Christ. Are the three persons of the Trinity eternal, co-existent, beings which are one with the First Cause, or is Deity a hierarchy of differentiated entities, parts of which are subordinate to the whole? Post-Nicene orthodoxy takes the former view. The Trinity is consubstantial, co-eternal. Likewise, in orthodox doctrine, the incarnate Jesus Christ was *both* 'fully a human being with a human soul' *and* eternally, from the beginning, 'fully one with the First Cause of the Creation'. Christ was thus one Person in two Natures. This doctrine has the direct implication that the Incarnation was a unique, once-for-all, non-rational, historical event which can never be repeated.

But the earlier Christians, as well as later schismatic opinion, diverged from this view in two directions. At one extreme it was held that Christ was always God and his human form only an appearance; at the other, the human Christ and the divine Logos, though housed in one fleshly body, were separate rather than fused. In either case, God, as such, has only one nature.

Monophysite doctrines of this latter kind have two important consequences. First they imply that there was a time when the incarnate Christ was not, and hence that He is in some sense, a specially created Being, secondary to the First Cause. But secondly they imply that any inspired human prophet who feels himself to be possessed by the Holy Spirit is really no different, in kind, from Christ himself. Hence the Incarnation ceases to be a unique historical event in the past; it becomes a perpetually repeatable event belonging to the present.

The particular heresy for which Arius was condemned in A.D. 325 was the doctrine that the Christ–Logos was a created being, which carried the implication that the Trinity is a hierarchy of separate persons of different degrees of efficacy. I am claiming that there is a logical 'fit' between the rejection of this doctrine and the acceptance of Imperialism and Episcopal hierarchy. Let me elaborate the kind of correlation I have in mind.

In any established political hierarchy the legitimacy of any individual office-holder's actions derives from the delegated authority of some other office-holder higher up the system. At the top of the pyramid the legitimacy of the actions of the Emperor-Pope can derive from one source only, the direct authority of God himself.

Wherever religion serves to support the established order in this way it must recognise a hierarchy of human beings and must approve of the order of time as it is now. The social world, as it is now and ever shall be, is ruled by men whose authority derives from a unique, remote, self-legitimising, eternal source, God. The common man can have no direct access to this ultimate power; his only approach is through the hierarchy of established *human* officers. There can be no short cuts. Any suggestion that the common man should expect further direct intervention by God in the ordering of society amounts to sedition, since it calls in question the legitimacy of the established order. It follows that all theories about the commencement of 'new time', or the imminent appearance of divine beings in human form, are politically subversive.

Catholic orthodoxy is consistent with this pattern. The Redemption of Mankind was a once-for-all event which occurred in the historical past and need not occur again. God and Jesus are one person in two natures, the completely Divine and the completely Human. There is no hierarchy of greater and lesser deities. There is one deity remote and unapproachable except through the mediation of a consecrated human priest, whose legitimacy of status was established from the beginning through the apostolic succession.

Where religion serves subversive ends the opposite pattern prevails. The present state of affairs is evil, but, with the triumph of the revolution, new time will commence. Since rebellion is clearly illegitimate in terms of the *existing* secular hierarchy, it must be made legitimate by taking short cuts to the ultimate divine source of power. It follows that the radical sectarian's God must be directly approachable by each individual whether he be a priest or not. Redemption is not something that has been granted to all mankind subject only to the obedience of the individual; it is a privilege of the Elect, the Saints who are individually in direct communication with God.

In the Christian version of this doctrine God the Son – the Christ–Logos – becomes a subordinate function of the Father but closer and more approachable. In effect, God the Son and God the Holy Spirit become demi-gods; but, equally, the spiritual leaders of men are themselves almost demi-gods since they are directly inspired by the Holy Spirit. Indeed there have been numerous radical egalitarian sects in which the postulated historical Jesus was rated as a kind of super-prophet rather

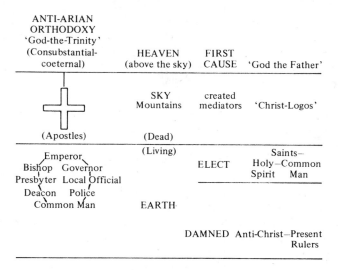

Figure 2. Deity–man hierarchy: alternative cosmological schema.

than a God and the whole congregation qualified individually for Saint-hood. Figure 2 illustrates this model schema. The left-hand column is intended to exemplify the structure of sixth-century dyophysite ortho-doxy in the reign of Justinian. The right-hand column is that of Arian millenarian heresy of the kind that was generally fashionable prior to A.D. 325. You will notice that it is the same diagram as that shown in Fig. 1 but tilted on one side: impotent man below, omnipotent God above, channel of mediation in between. In the left-hand column the channel of mediation is the sacrificial cross; on the right it is the demi-god Christ–Logos.

Now in structuralist theory the geometry of cosmological ideas is their most fundamental characteristic; so my argument becomes a testable hypothesis. If my diagram is a 'correct' structural representation of the difference between orthodoxy and Arianism then it should show up in the iconographic conventions of early Christianity. Let us see where we can get to with that one!

Not perhaps very far. In order to demonstrate such a thesis I should need to have *certain* evidence about the iconographic conventions of second-century Christianity. I do not have that evidence. Early Christian art was probably very limited in quantity. Many of the Fathers, like their seventeenth-century Puritan successors, considered that all 'images were demonic symbols of superstition' (Chadwick 1967: 277 ff.). It is true that right from the start Christianity had its wealthy patrons who may have decorated their private houses with Christian themes, but direct evidence of this has not survived. So long as Christianity remained an illegal cult there can have been no public churches. We know that fourth-century churches existed in fair number and that they were lavishly decorated, but very little of this art now survives (Beckwith 1970: 10–11). It follows that all the theories about the iconographic conventions of very early Christianity are highly speculative. However it may plausibly be argued that where a datable early fifth-century mosaic contains an apparently 'established' convention, or repeats some theme of which there is an isolated instance in an earlier tomb painting from the catacombs, it is likely that the fifth-century picture derives from an original belonging to the fourth century or earlier.

That is an extremely tight summary of a very complex argument but it must suffice. This is where Melchisedech comes into my story.

Melchisedech is a figure of considerable importance in the non-canonical literature of both sectarian Judaism and early Christianity. In the Qumran literature he is equated with the Archangel Michael as Judge of the Last Days (Van der Woude 1965) and is prominent in various apocalyptic Christian tracts such as *The Book of Adam and Eve* and *The Slavonic Book of Enoch* which have their ultimate origin in pre-Christian originals of the first century A.D. Although the total 'apocryphal mythology' of Melchisedech is considerable, relatively little attention seems to have been paid to him after the sixth century, though in modern times he has a place in Mormon doctrine. In the early literature millenarianism and Melchisedech seem to be closely associated. It would seem that he was only infrequently represented in early Church art and only three major pictorial representations have survived from antiquity. They are shown together in Plates 1, 2 and 3.

All three illustrations refer to the same passage in Genesis 14, which reads as follows:

> And Melchisedech king of Salem brought forth bread and wine: and he was the priest of the most high God. And he blessed him, and said 'Blessed be Abram of the most high God, possessor of heaven and earth; and blessed be the most high God, which hath delivered thine enemies into thy hand'. And Abram gave him tithes of all.

In accordance with the principle of the recapitulation of time the early Christian Fathers treated this incident as a prefiguration of the Eucharist.

It is clear that the three pictures exemplify two quite different iconographic conventions. In Plate 1, Melchisedech presents bread and wine to Abraham as in the Genesis quotation. The Christ–Logos floats overhead in human form pointing at Melchisedech. There is no altar or other ritual paraphernalia.

In Plates 2 and 3, we only know that we are dealing with Melchisedech because he is so named. God is off-stage and points at the scene with a three-fingered hand projecting through the sky. Melchisedech is explicitly the priest at the Eucharist, engaged in a ritual involving an altar.

The two pictures containing the Hand of God and the Altar can be given a precise context. They come from Ravenna in the time of Justinian. The picture with the floating Christ–Logos is more uncertain. It is one of the mosaic panels in the nave of the church of Santa Maria Maggiore in Rome. There are now twenty-five such panels though formerly there were more. They show scenes from the life of Abraham on one side and from the lives of Moses and Joshua on the other. All the panels have been mutilated and brutally restored at various times. For the past seventy years there has been an impassioned and immensely learned debate about the dating and provenance of these panels which still continues. The present consensus of learned opinion seems to be that the mosaics are of the same date as the main fabric of the church itself, which can be dated fairly precisely to around A.D. 432. Earlier experts had maintained that the pictures were a hang-over from a much earlier building. However, there appears to be agreement that where these panels reflect a peculiar convention of their own this must be a survival from an earlier period. The floating Christ–Logos figure in Plate 1 is one such peculiarity. It appears in five different places in the twenty-five surviving panels whereas the Hand of God convention, which is elsewhere quite common, appears only once.[9]

There seems to be substantial agreement that, whatever may be the date of the panels themselves, the floating Christ–Logos refers back to the kind of argument that was presented by Justin Martyr in the second century where he argues at great length that the 'Creator of all things Who always remains above the heavens and Who has never been seen by any man' is to be distinguished from the God who appeared to Abraham, Moses and Joshua who was 'another God and Lord *under* the Creator of all things, in that He bears messages to men, whatever the Creator, above whom there is no other God, wills to be borne to them' (Justin: Dialogue with Trypho 56).

By the early fifth century this hierarchical Arian view of the mediating deity was already thoroughly heretical; the orthodox view would have been that of St Augustine ((a) Ch. 10: 68); 'In so far as Christ is man, he is mediator but not in so far as He is Word, for as such he is co-equal with God.' But it would seem that the artists of Santa Maria Maggiore had not managed to keep up to date with the latest shifts in theology.

The two Ravenna pictures come from the churches of San Vitale and San Apollinare in Classe. Both churches are of the same date; they were dedicated in 548 and 549 respectively. Their decorations commemorated the reassertion of full Byzantine authority over Italy after half a century during which the Ostrogothic kingdom founded by Theodoric had been more or less independent. The Ostrogoths were Christians of mildly Arian persuasion and Ravenna was their capital. In 543 Justinian had taken a personal lead in declaring that the teaching of Origen in the third century had been heretical and a precursor of Arianism. It was thus appropriate that the new churches, designed to do honour to Justinian, should be filled with explicit anti-Arian propaganda. The iconography in question has in fact been interpreted in this sense (Quitt 1903).

The original decorations of San Vitale are fairly complete. They include portraits of the Emperor Justinian and the Empress Theodora and their courts [Plates 4 and 5]. Notice that Justinian and Theodora are distinguished by halos. They are living saints, near deities. Over the vault of the apse is a beardless Christ in the role of World Emperor [Plate 6]. Here again the implication is that the Emperor is a mediator in a special class by himself.

Apart from these glorifications of the Emperor himself and of the divine sanction of his imperial role the two principal panels are representations of sacrifice. In my language they are icons of orthodoxy [Plates 7 and 2].

Plate 7 on the left shows Abraham offering hospitality to the three Angels, (representing the Trinity), who have come to announce the impending pregnancy of Sarah, extreme left. On the right Abraham prepares to sacrifice Isaac, the son born of that pregnancy. The three-fingered hand of God reaches through the heavens to deter him. Far right Moses receives the commandments direct from the hand of God while inferior commoner Israelites chatter below.

The corresponding panel on the other side of the aisle is the one you have already seen in Plate 2. Abel emerges from a hut and offers a lamb; Melchisedech with a halo emerges from his kingly palace and offers bread and wine from an altar. God is again represented by a hand piercing the sky. On the left is another representation of Moses, this time communicating direct with the deity on high through the burning bush. The commoner Israelites have here been reduced to the status of sheep.

Abel is of course another 'prefiguration'. He is the son of Adam who *first* offers a lamb as sacrifice and is *then* himself slain; he 'prefigured' the Crucifixion considered as the sacrifice of Jesus, the Son of God—Lamb of God. Conversely Isaac the son of Abraham is *first* offered as a sacrifice, and *then* replaced at the last minute by the 'ram caught in a thicket'. Melchisedech as the priest of the Eucharist is thus quite logically associated with both these prefigurations of the Crucifixion. The mythological equations are that Abel equals Jesus as the son who is himself sacrificed, while Melchisedech equals Abraham as the Priest who makes an offering symbolic of the sacrifice of the son. But he is also the Emperor with his halo.

The Melchisedech picture from the S. Apollinare in Classe [Plate 3] combines elements from the two panels we have just seen. Abel, the Lamb, Abraham and Isaac, the Altar, the Bread and Wine. Melchisedech and the Hand of God. Melchisedech has now however moved behind the altar and sits in a position appropriate to a representation of Jesus Christ breaking bread at the Last Supper. Taken in combination with the previous pictures there is a complete elision of all the mediator-priest-sacrificer figures: Abel equals Abraham equals Melchisedech equals Jesus Christ.

But notice that there is no actual representation of Jesus Christ; he forms part of the equation only by implication because of Melchisedech's role as priest of the Eucharist. Deity is only explicitly represented as the three-fingered Hand of God piercing the sky and as the three undifferentiated angels sitting close together.[10]

In other words God is present in two natures as the Divine Trinity above the sky and as Priest–Victim–Human Being on earth. There is no hierarchy of superhuman mediators, but there is a hierarchy between human mediator and human commoner – Moses in relation to the Israelites, Abraham in relation to Sarah and Isaac.

Notice how this arrangement contrasts with the Roman picture which I discussed earlier [Plate 1]. Here as you see Melchisedech is offering food and wine to Abraham; he is *not* making a sacrifice to God on High. There is no altar, no background of ritual gadgets, no reference to the Trinity, no royal regalia, no hierarchy between mediator and human commoner. The direct equation is between the bread and the wine in the lower part of the picture and the Christ–Logos in the upper part. Abraham as communicant and Melchisedech as priest have equal standing.[11]

But what is all this about? As I have indicated, the non-canonical mythology of Melchisedech is extensive but for present purposes it will suffice if we stick to the Bible proper, where he is named on only three occasions. I have already given you the Genesis quotation where, you will recall, he was described as 'King of Salem and Priest of the Most High God'. This story was taken to be not only the first reference to a prefigured Eucharist but also the first reference to Jerusalem. This made it a highly appropriate millenarian symbol of new time and the New Jerusalem.

The second mention of Melchisedech comes in Psalm 110 where the King sits at God's right hand as the judge over the wicked and is declared to be 'a priest for ever after the order of Melchisedech'. On this account the sect of the Qumran community looked upon Melchisedech as the judge of the last days and gave him a supernatural mediator status as Archangel.

The third Biblical reference comes from the New Testament, but implies a knowledge of Philo's Hellenistic commentary on Genesis written about A.D. 30 where Melchisedech's title of 'King of Salem' is glossed to mean 'King of Peace'. On this basis that Psalmist's reference to the King in his role of 'Priest for ever after the order of Melchisedech' would signify that he is King of Peace as well as King of Justice and Righteousness. This makes Melchisedech a very appropriate symbol for a Christian Roman Emperor.

In the New Testament Epistle to the Hebrews, the three passages to which I have referred from Genesis, Psalms and Philo are elaborated into a homily which extends over seven chapters.

Melchisedech is described as a being 'without father, without mother, without descent, having neither beginning of days, nor end of life; but made like unto the Son of God; abideth a priest for ever'. Jesus is 'the apostle and high priest of our confession' and hence is to be equated with the Psalmist's King who was 'a priest for ever after the order of Melchisedech', a role which is contrasted with that of temporary mortal priests 'of the order of Aaron'.

It should be immediately apparent that the Biblical texts lend themselves to a variety of interpretation. If for example Melchisedech King of Salem is Prince of Peace he can serve to support conservative attitudes, but if he is King of the New Jerusalem he is a revolutionary.

It also seems fairly evident that the Roman and Ravenna artists were exploiting different possibilities. But now look again at Fig. 2. When I first showed you this diagram I suggested that it could be taken to represent Arian doctrine on the right and orthodox doctrine on the left. Compare the middle section of the right-hand column with the Roman picture [Plate 1]. The priest is the channel through whom the charisma of the Christ–Logos is transferred to the bread and wine. The Christ–Logos is visibly present in the immediate situation and is clearly distinguished from the human priest. On the other hand priest and communicant are on the same level. Now look at the left-hand column of my diagram (Fig. 2), the schema which represents mediation through sacrifice, and compare it with the Ravenna pictures [Plates 2, 3 and 7]. Notice again how God is invisible above the sky and present only as a hand. This hand points at Melchisedech who poses as the Christ of the Last Supper. He is surely the King of Peace, Righteousness and Justice and a type for Justinian? Though plainly labelled Melchisedech he is Christ in his human nature. Notice too the change of context. Melchisedech is still the priest of the Eucharist but he is now making a sacrifice to a High God from an altar adorned with ritual trappings and he emerges from a palace.

Where the Roman picture might depict a meeting of Quakers or Congregationalists, Ravenna's Melchisedech plainly lives in a world of Bishops and Cathedrals.

The point I have been making is given even more marked emphasis in the apse of S. Apollinare in Classe, the church containing the seated Melchisedech. Here again there is repetition of hierarchy among the human beings but a careful avoidance of any representation of hierarchy among the deities. Plate 8 shows the apse in question. Right at the top we have a three-layered universe, with the layers sharply differentiated. First Christ himself boxed in a circle; then the four Evangelists in their symbolic form in the sky, then the sheep emerging from the walled cities of Jerusalem and Bethlehem.

In the apse proper the design as a whole appears to refer obliquely to both the Transfiguration and the Ascension. At the very top we again have the three-fingered Hand of God pointing at a cross, boxed in a circle, with Christ's head boxed in another circle right at the centre of the cross. On either side of the sky are Elias and Moses. The world below is sharply separated and is dominated by the human figure of St Apollinaris[12] who is very large in comparison with his sheep who are themselves arranged in hierarchy.

The three elevated sheep, two on one side and one on the other are said to be Peter, James and John who were present at the Transfiguration. Here one suspects they represent the Pope of Rome and two of the eastern Patriarchs.

But the relevant point is the 'iconoclastic' cross (Beckwith 1970: 54). The artist has gone out of his way to make the Christ figure identical with God on High and to make him seem remote and inaccessible. There is no floating Logos in the sky; there is no explicit God-on-Earth accessible to ordinary men. In the iconography as a whole the identity of the Divine Emperor and of 'Christ as Man' become confused, but there is no ambiguity about the separation between kingly priests and their sheep.

The total implication is rather surprising, or at any rate I found it so: *visible hierarchy among deities goes with egalitarian politics among men; isolated monotheism goes with hierarchical politics among men.*[13]

Second-century Melchisedech was a man of the people; sixth-century Melchisedech was a Priest-King in an imperial autocracy.

This change in iconographic convention corresponds to a real-world shift in the political acceptability of Christianity which accompanied its progression from the inchoate creed of an underworld minority to the formal orthodoxy of a state religion.

I find it interesting that the 'model' that emerges from a study of the iconography should be essentially the same as the model which emerges as the outcome of sociological analysis. An equation of this sort could well have implications for our understanding of contemporary events as well as those of ancient history.

Let me recapitulate. I have drawn attention on two contrasted theologies. One of these can serve to support the legitimacy of an established hierarchical political authority, the other is appropriate for an under-privileged minority seeking justification for rebellion against established authority. I have made the point that these are not just polar attitudes but dialectical attitudes. The heirs and successors of the advocates of revo-lution become the upholders of the legitimate establishment. I have argued that this is what happened to Western Christianity between the second and sixth centuries A.D. The whole proliferation of rival doctrines can be classed as belonging to one or other of two wide-spread but polar types – Arian and monophysite on the one side; anti-Arian and dyophysite on the other. The Arians, with rare exceptions, consistently support local autonomy and stand opposed to the centralised regime; the anti-Arians support it.

In this context I have used the three illustrations of Melchisedech for two purposes, first to show that the shift of iconographic convention corresponds to my thesis, and secondly to show that the iconographic conventions themselves have a visual structure which is already implicit in the form of my verbal argument.

But another aspect of my thesis should not be overlooked. As the heretics of one generation move up the social scale and become respect-able they become indistinguishable from the established orthodoxy at the top, but that leaves a gap at the bottom within which new millenarian, anarchist, egalitarian heresies will constantly be generated.

Let me commend to you an article by Baden Hickman, published in *The Guardian* on the 19 August 1972, entitled 'A schism of isms'. It is concerned with the proliferation of 'small unconventional Christian sects' mainly among the lower working-class immigrant population. Hickman notes that in this country there are now over eighty distinct denominations and perhaps 400 or more sectarian congregations. They

84

have titles such as The New Testament Church of God, The Church of God of Prophecy, The Apostolic Church of Jesus Christ. 'Periodical disintegration of the various sects seems to do nothing to lessen their fervour. New groupings can be formed overnight.' One anonymous group regularly forms groups of twelve apostles only to disband. Each of the twelve is then commissioned to form a new group of twelve, and so on . . . 'This', remarks Hickman, 'is an old "cell" technique used by Marxists and traditional evangelical churchmen . . . ' I quote again: 'The attitude of the sects to their white Church neighbours is usually one of smiling politeness. This hides the truth; most of these black Christians see the white Churchgoers as hell bent . . . they believe that their white brothers and sisters are ignoring, among other things, the power and presence of the Holy Spirit.'

'Small unconventional Christian sects' they, are, but that is where Christianity began, at the bottom, in a mood of political dissent. Even non-Christian social anthropologists can, I believe, profit by reflecting on such matters.

Notes

1 Kelly 1958: 23; cf. Cullmann (1967); Brox (1971); Schoeps (1956). For a modern statement of the orthodox view that early Christianity was a unitary church, see Frend (1965).

2 Marx and Engels (1957) is an anthology of miscellaneous sources compiled by Soviet editors. Few of the items bear directly on the theme of religion. In general, Marx and Engels seem to have held that *in the circumstances of nineteenth-century capitalism* religious belief functioned as a drug which inhibited the working class from achieving full class consciousness and deceived the bourgeoisie into thinking that their interests were those of the ruling class. However, Engels also maintained that the rapid success of early Christianity provides historical evidence that religion may fill a different function under conditions of slavery. In a remarkable passage in 'On the history of early Christianity' (1895) (Marx and Engels 1957: 313) he declares that there is a direct parallel between the rise of Christianity in the second century A.D. and the rise of revolutionary socialism in the nineteenth century. The fact that in less than 300 years after its first appearance Christianity had become the state religion of the Roman World Empire 'makes the victory of socialism absolutely certain'.

In short, Engels' Marxism was itself a millenarian cult. He devotes considerable effort to the cabbalistic decipherment of the Book of Revelation, 'proving' among other things that the number 666, 'the mark on the Beast', is a cipher for the name of the Emperor Nero. In another passage in the same essay (p. 327) he draws a direct parallel between the sectarianism of nineteenth-century socialism and the sectarianism of early Christianity.

3 This generalisation has been challenged – e.g. by Cohn (1962), but is, I believe, broadly defensible. However, there are cases where members of an effete ruling class threatened by imminent loss of influence have resorted to millenarian

prophets. Trotsky was inclined to explain the influence of Rasputin in this way (cf. Shepperson 1962: 46).

4 St Ignatius always described himself as 'God inspired' (cf. Richardson 1953: 74–120). Note Richardson's own comment (p. 76): 'the bishop in Ignatius is not only an administrator and liturgical officer; he is also a prophet'.

5 Beckwith 1970: Plate 9 – 'Rome, catacomb painting mid fourth century'. Compare the mosaic panel on the same theme in Santa Maria Maggiore (? early fifth century) (Cecchelli 1956: Plate xxxi).

Early Christian treatment of Old Testament themes was probably an adaptation of conventions first established in decorated Jewish synagogues. See Chadwick 1967: 279 and various sources listed by Beckwith 1970:168; see also Bianchi-Bandinelli 1955.

6 E.g. Donatism: see Frend 1952: 203.

7 Augustine (b) XX: Chs 3–29. There is evidence that outside the main centres of political and Church authority millenarian ideas persisted well into the fifth century: cf. Frend 1965: 563, n. 31.

8 Dodgson 1854: 129 citing Augustine. Note in this respect the distinction made by Shepperson (1962: 44) between post-millennial and pre-millennial doctrines.

9 The best complete set of illustrations is in Cecchelli (1956). It needs to be borne in mind however that these pictures are based on photographs taken *after* the latest series of 'restorations' which were carried out under Papal direction during the 1920s. There have been substantial changes in some of the panels even since the beginning of this century. For a recent survey of the dating argument see Oakeshott (1967). See also Bianchi-Bandinelli (1955:146–8 and references at p. 146 n. 2).

10 This part of the picture is closely related to one of the panels in the S. Maria Maggiore series. However in the latter Abraham expressly makes his offering to the central 'angel'. In another scene on the same panel the central angel is enclosed in a nimbus implying an hierarchical conception of the Trinity. See Cecchelli 1956: Plate XV and comment at pp. 106–7.

11 The whole of the right side of the picture has been ruthlessly restored on several occasions and its original form is in doubt. Richter and Taylor (1904) suggested that Abraham was originally on foot.

12 This Apollinarius (Apollinaris) is a local Ravenna saint and not Apollinarius of Laodicea, the fourth-century theologian associated with the Apollinarian heresy.

13 Chadwick's comment that the growth of popular Mariolatry originally represented a Monophysite reaction to Dyophysite Orthodoxy is relevant here: popular Monophysite Christology of the fifth Century transferred to St Mary the redemptive value that had been attributed to the humanity of Christ. In a Monophysite devotion Christ as man ceased to be very important; his resurrection was that of a God. Because of this loss of a sense of solidarity between Christ and the human race, the faithful increasingly looked towards Mary as the perfect representative redeemed humanity (Chadwick 1967: 282).

References

Augustine, Saint (S. Aurelii Augustini). *a.* Confessions; *b.* De civitate Dei.

Beckwith, John 1970 *Early Christian and Byzantine art*, Harmondsworth: Penguin

Bianchi-Bandinelli, R. 1955 *Hellenistic-Byzantine Miniatures of the Ilias Ambrosiana*, Olten: Urs Graf Verlag

Brox, N. 1971 'Forms of Christianity in the primitive church', *Concilium* 7, 33–46

Cecchelli, C. 1956 *I mosaici della basilica di S. Maria Maggiore*, Turin: Ilte

Chadwick, H. 1967 *The Early Church*, Harmondsworth: Penguin

Clement. The letter of the Church of Rome to the Church of Corinth, commonly called Clement's First Letter. See Richardson 1953: 33–73

Cohn, N. 1957 *The Pursuit of the Millennium*, London: Secker & Warburg
     1962 'Medieval millenarism: its bearing on the comparative study of millenarian movements', in *Millennial Dreams in Action* (ed.) S. L. Thrupp, The Hague: Mouton.

Cullmann, O. 1967 'La diversité des types de Christianisme dans l'Eglise primitive', *Stud. Mat. Storia Relig.* 38, 175–84

Dodgson, C. (trans.) 1854 *Tertullian*, Oxford: Parker

Firth, R. 1964 'Problem and assumption in the anthropological study of religion', in *Essays on Social Organization and Values*, London: Athlone

Frend, W. H. C. 1952 The Donatist Church: a movement of protest in Roman north Africa
     1965 *Martyrdom and Persecution in the early Christian Church*, Oxford: Blackwell

Hickman, B. 1972 'A schism of isms', *The Guardian* 19 August, 1972

Hill, Christopher 1972 *The World Turned Upside Down*, London: Temple Smith

Hobsbawm, E. 1959 *Primitive Rebels: Studies in Archaic Forms of Social Movement in the 19th and 20th centuries*, Manchester

Justin, 1861 *The Works Now Extant of S. Justin the Martyr*, Oxford: J. H. & J. Parker

Kelly, J. N. D. 1958 *Early Christian Doctrines*, London: A. & C. Black

Lamont, W. 1972 'Richard Baxter, the Apocalypse and the Mad Major', *Past & Present* 55, 58–90

Lanternari, V. 1963 *The Religions of the Oppressed*, London: MacGibbon & Kee

Marx, K. & F. Engels 1957 *On Religion*, Moscow: Foreign Languages Publishing House

Oakeshott, Walter, F. 1967 *The Mosaics of Rome*, London: Thames & Hudson

Quitt, J. 1903 'Die Mosaiken von S. Vitale in Ravenna: eine Apologie des Dyophysitismus aus dem VI. Jahrhunderten', *Byzantische Denkmäler* 3, 71–109

Richardson, C. C. 1953 *Early Christian Fathers*, London: S.C.M. Press

Richter, J. P. & Cameron Taylor 1904 *The Golden Age of Classic Christian Art*, London: Duckworth

Schoeps, H.-J. 1956 *Urgemeinde Judenchristentum Gnosis*, Tübingen: J.C.B. Mohr

Shepperson, G. 1962 'The comparative study of millenarian movements', in *Millennial Dreams in Action* (ed.) S. L. Thrupp, The Hague: Mouton

Thrupp, Sylvia L. (ed.) 1962 *Millennial Dreams in Action* (Comp. Stud. Soc. Hist. Suppl. 2), The Hague: Mouton

Van der Woude, A. S. 1965 'Melchisedek als himmlische Erlösergestalt in den neugenfundenen eschatologischen Midrashim aud Qmran-Höhle', *Oudtest. Stud.* 14, 354–73

Weber, Max 1947 *The Theory of Social and Economic Organization* (trans.)
A. R. Henderson & Talcott Parsons, London: William Hodge
Worsley, P. 1957 *The Trumpet Shall Sound: a Study of Cargo Cults in Melanesia,*
London

1 Melchisedech presents bread and wine to Abraham. Santa Maria
Maggiore, Rome.

2 S. Vitale, Ravenna. Matching panel to Plate 8.

3 S. Apollinare in Classe, Ravenna.

4 Justinian and courtiers. Note the halo. S. Vitale, Ravenna.

5 Theodora and court. Note the halo. S. Vitale, Ravenna.

6 Christ as World Emperor. S. Vitale, Ravenna, main apse.

7 S. Vitale, Ravenna. Matching panel to Plate 2.

8 Main apse, S. Apollinare in Classe, Ravenna.

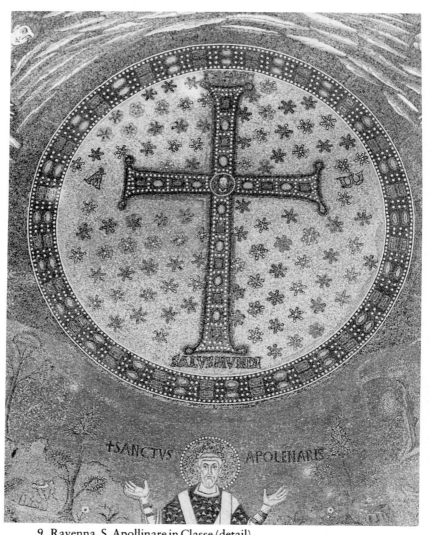

9 Ravenna, S. Apollinare in Classe (detail).

5 Against genres: are parables lights set in candlesticks or put under a bushel?*

EDMUND LEACH

As was anticipated, this lecture, in the context of its original delivery, had a mixed reception. The amateurs and some of the literary critics were favourably impressed, the theologians were dismissive. But it would appear that both sides misunderstood my general thinking about the relationship between sacred texts and ritual performance. The first few pages of the present version are intended to clarify this personal issue.

My anthropological experience has been varied. It has included field research among the Kachins of North Burma, the Iban of Borneo and Sinhalese Buddhists in Sri Lanka.

In the pre-colonial era the North Burma Kachin operated with oral not written traditions. Their religious texts were immense saga-length poems delivered on set occasions by professional experts. The 'story' which they contained was expandable. According to the dignity of the occasion (and to the scale of the saga-teller's fee) the performance might last for anything from half an hour or so to several days. But, whether expanded or shrunk, it was always much the same story. The saga as a whole contained, as it were, a number of main chapters and cross-headings. Sections of story text corresponding to these various headings were always present though some might be much abbreviated and the sequence of the telling was not invariably the same.

Among the Iban of Borneo the position was similar except that there was a more clear-cut notion of what constituted a story unit. The saga-tellers thumped out the rhythm of their poems with the aid of a pole on which was marked a series of rectangular ideograms. Each ideogram was a mnemonic for a particular section of the main story but each section could be expanded or shrunk according to circumstance. There was no fixed 'authentic text'.

With the Buddhist Sinhalese things are rather different. The monks have access to a huge corpus of literary texts, much of which they learn

*A public lecture given on January 6, 1982, as part of a Seminar Conference organised by the British Comparative Literature Association on the theme of: 'Parable and Narrative Form in the Bible and Literature'

off by heart. *Pirit* ceremonies which may continue for many hours entail the intoned recitation of such texts. In this case it is not just a matter of repeating a more or less standard story in a fairly free-wheeling style, the words themselves are sacred. Deviation from the details of the written text are not allowed. But in this case, since it is impossible to give 'the whole story', the total text has to be cut up into sections appropriate to particular occasions.

Modern English Protestant Christian practice is different again. There are very few occasions when long sections of the gospel text are read out continuously; it is usually served up only in short 'lessons' distributed throughout the year. Except at special Festivals such as Christmas and Easter there seems to be little attempt to place associated stories from the Old and New Testament or from different gospels in close conjunction. In ritual performance, such as in the Eucharist, the main gospel text is referred to only by metonymic association through short quotation, though such citations are synecdochic representations of the larger whole. It seems to be assumed that each individual member of the congregation will know 'the whole story' as a result of his/her education or private reading. In the Protestant tradition enormous value is attached to the exact wording of the 'original' text, even if in fact the text in question is a sixteenth-Century English version of a Latin Text translated from the Greek and Hebrew.

This last feature however differs from Jewish attitudes. The fact that the Old-Testament biblical canon was fully established in the first or second Century B.C. did not inhibit later Rabbinical preachers from adding decorative details out of their own imagination just to add human interest or give emphasis to a particular moral implication.

As far as I can discover no one knows very much about the details of early Christian ritual practice or of Jewish ritual practice in the first and second Centuries A.D. Since Christianity clearly started out as a sect within Judaism, with close parallels in the rather earlier Qumran community and in the gnostic sects which later came to be treated as heresies from Christianity itself, the practices of these 'analogous' sects, if we knew what they were, would be relevant for our understanding of the earliest Christian materials. We do not know what they were but there are some fragmentary bits of contemporary evidence. One such bit of evidence is provided by the surviving paintings on the walls of the Dura-Europos synagogue which can be firmly dated to the early years of the third Century A.D.

In an extremely valuable survey of the diverse opinions which have been expressed concerning Dura-Europos, Gutmann (1973) remarks that: '[3rd Century] Dura belongs to a radically new type of Judaism that had emerged much earlier, out of which Christianity grew and was

90

nourished. This new Judaism had substituted prayers within synagogues for sacrifices at the Temple. It offered eternal life through personal salvation and bodily resurrection, rather than promising fertility of the land' (pp. 144–5).

Gutmann's problem in this essay is that the Dura panels, all of which depict identifiable scenes from the Old Testament, are not arranged in any order which ties in with 'their original narrative sequence'. His conclusion is that these pictures are not simply illustrations of a mishmash of Old-Testament stories but rather that they were 'used simply as prooftexts with the purpose of driving home ... a new theological concept, liturgy or teaching'.

Gutmann sees parallels between this use of Old-Testament iconography and that employed in Santa Maria Maggiore in Rome and San Vitale in Ravenna which, while later than Dura, are among the earliest large-scale sets of Christian illustrations still surviving. In particular, Gutmann makes the comment that: 'In such churches as S. Vitale, Ravenna, we know that the main function of the building and its art was to give meaning to the "liturgy of the Eucharist"' (p. 146).

In the case of the S. Vitale mosaics it is transparently clear that this is in fact the case. The argument that lies at the back of my present essay is that the apparently episodic text of the gospels should likewise be seen as a unity which gives meaning to the liturgy of the Eucharist.

The earliest Christians had no church buildings, and archaeology has so far produced extremely few objects of any kind which are of unambiguously Christian origin and of a date prior to the third Century. And this is not surprising. In warning the Christians against image-making, Clement and Tertullian appear to have been more concerned with practical dangers than with impiety. But Finney (1977) argues convincingly that it is most unlikely that the early Christians were strictly aniconic. What is likely to have happened is that the Christians used politically acceptable Jewish and Classical symbols but gave these symbols their own (secret) meaning. The 'Good Shepherd' was one such familiar image which could be assimilated to the Christian story. There were many others.

But what I am suggesting is that, precisely because the earliest Christians were greatly restricted in the extent to which they could risk using visual imagery, they developed a sacred literature in which the narrative is peculiarly pictorial and episodic. The 'episodes' are likely to have been used in the way the picture panels in third-Century Dura and sixth-Century Ravenna were used: 'to give meaning to the liturgy'.

When, as an anthropologist, I refer to the New Testament as 'myth', this is what I have in mind.

[The next few paragraphs formed part of the lecture as delivered, but were added at the last minute so as to clarify my stance with regard to various issues that had arisen during the earlier Conference discussions.]

Let me emphasise right from the start that I am in no way concerned with authors' intentions. I do not believe that one can discriminate between correct and incorrect 'interpretations' of biblical texts. In that field there are no limits to fantasy. Of course each of us finds some of those fantasies more attractive or more plausible than others; but I would categorically deny that there can be a *correct* version.

My purpose in this lecture is to demonstrate the existence of a thematic pattern in certain well known biblical texts. I show (within the limits of time available) that the same thematic patterning is repeated with variations in the different gospels.

When you have heard what I have to say, there are a variety of possible reactions. For example, you might say: 'Yes I knew that but it is an uninteresting accident.' Or you might say: 'Well I must admit I hadn't noticed that, it does look significant.' Between those two extremes there are a wide range of other possibilities.

But if I persuade some of you that the patterns in question are not accidental, then what about 'intention'? Surely a non-accidental pattern must be an intentional pattern?

But that is not my position.

I have no idea how the gospels came to be written, but I do know (or think I know) that at least from an early date in the second Century A.D. texts very similar to those we now know were being used in Christian services. I assume that this context of use had an influence on the way the texts were arranged and at least in some degree on the actual content of the texts as such.

It seems to me absolutely impossible that any form of modern exegesis could show just what this influence was. And from my point of view it doesn't in the least matter. By the time the canon was fully established the context of use was already 'part of the text'. I am not concerned with what a hypothetical living Jesus might or might not have really said.

I am not arguing that the ordering of text to fit ritual needs was a conscious manipulation by individuals. Intention does not come into it. But I am saying that if, as I believe, the structured patterning of these texts now conveys a religious message, that message is inseparable from the religious ideology of the early church in which these texts were first used.

92

This in no way precludes the possibility, indeed the likelihood, that there are other levels of meaning in the text which can be discovered either by straight aesthetic intuition or by the various procedures of complex exegetical analysis in which academic theologians delight.

But now for the lecture proper.

Let me start by briefly explaining my title. The ordinary theological exegesis of the New Testament assumes that the texts of the gospels as we now have them can be broken down into materials of several different kinds. In particular, there are passages which purport to record sequences of historical events and there are passages which record the verbal teaching that Jesus delivered in the course of those events. Parables form a sub-class of the passages embodying verbal teaching.

The thesis which I am maintaining on the present occasion is that this kind of fragmentation of the textual materials into genres of different kinds is radically misleading. Text is text. We shall only understand the text as a whole if we recognise that some sections are structural transformations of other sections. But these transformations cut right across the conventional genre-distinctions to which I have referred.

In any case the genre-distinctions are much less precise than many people suppose.

I hardly have to remind an audience such as this that words which have entered the English language as translations or transcriptions of Greek or Latin terms which appear in Holy Writ have acquired a very special quality of their own. Everyone has the impression that such words have clear, easily defined, even divinely ordained, meanings, but when you look into the matter you find that no two authorities can agree as to just what these meanings are. The word 'parable' is a case in point.

In Aristotle, *parabole* means 'comparison' or 'analogy', an argument of the form 'A is like B'. Many New-Testament parables have this superficial form but, in the Old Testament, 'parable' is the equivalent of Hebrew *mashal*, a word which has a whole range of meanings which the pedantic will distinguish as 'proverbs', 'fables', 'allegories', 'homilies', 'aphorisms', and so on. There are passages in the Old Testament which resemble New-Testament parables, but usually they are not so described. Biblical scholars have always been aware of these complexities but most of the more formidable experts end up by distinguishing a 'technical sense' of parable which makes it into a special genre of which the type-form is to be found in certain of the sayings of Jesus and which expressly excludes proverbs, fables and allegories. This creates difficulties all round. Some of these are very obvious.

If we go outside Christianity to look for sets of stories which embody homiletic teaching more or less in the New-Testament parable style, the closest parallels are, as one might expect, the Rabbinical parables which date from the early centuries of the Christian era, but, beyond that, the first examples that come to mind are the Buddhist Jataka Stories which purport to be concerned with events in the lives of previous incarnations of the Buddha.

Although none of the 547 stories in question is directly equivalent in content or structure to any of the New-Testament parables, the general form and the apparent moral implication are in many cases very similar. But many Jataka stories are stories in which animals talk and give moral advice; indeed a number of the Jataka stories are virtually identical to items in the Greek collection known as Aesop's Fables. So, if we accept the orthodox Christian view that parables are all plain tales about ordinary human beings, Jataka Stories are not parables.

But the 'plain tales' limitation raises another kind of difficulty. Jataka Stories do not have a commentary; their moral implication is held to be self-evident. To the modern reader this also appears to be the case for 'typical' New-Testament parables; on the face of it they would be readily comprehensible without the explanatory glosses with which they are often associated in the gospel text. These glosses make it appear as if the Christian parables were intended to be allegories. But according to Professor Nineham (Nineham 1963: 125–31), Rabbinical parables belonging to the Christian era are likewise self-evident in their apparent implication and they are not accompanied by any explanatory commentary.[1]

Nineham has claimed that this was also generally the case with Hebrew *mashal* at a much earlier period. He maintains that the three references to parables (*mashal*) in Ezekiel (where the word refers quite specifically to obscure allegories) are exceptional.

In elaborating this theme Nineham also asserts that 'although a *mashal* in Our Lord's time was not *intended* to be obscure, its meaning was essentially bound up with its original context and the circumstances of its utterance'. Just how he can know that obscurity was not intended is not revealed.

Nineham admits that some parable-like passages in the gospels now appear both obscure and inappropriate but claims that this is only because the original context of utterance has been lost. As examples of such 'parables', 'whose original context, and therefore meaning had become completely obscure by the time of the Evangelists', he cites the phrase about casting pearls before swine in Matthew 7.6 and the apparently inappropriate reference to eagles (vultures) gathering at a dead body in Matthew 24.28 and Luke 17.37. I can only say that I find Nineham's argument (and also his examples) most surprising.

In any case, anyone who adopts Nineham's view that New-Testament parables had an original context in which they were intended to have plain rather than allegorical meanings is faced with the difficulty that all three of the synoptic gospels assert precisely the opposite. It is specifically stated in the text that parables are mysteries the meaning of which is revealed to the Elect but which the multitude cannot understand.

Nineham himself gets out of this difficulty by saying that Mark 4.10–12 (and the equivalent passages Matthew 13.10–17 and Luke 10.23f.) represent a process of allegorisation introduced by the early Church rather than a part of the original teaching of Jesus. He claims that 'most scholars are agreed about this'. By 'most scholars' he presumably means professional Christian scholars like himself.

From my own highly sceptical point of view it seems absurd to attempt to distinguish, within our present gospel texts, between passages which are a direct transcription of the actual words of a real person, Jesus of Nazareth, and other passages which represent later editorial glosses on those actual words.

I would have supposed that it was perfectly obvious that we have no 'actual words'. What we have are four interrelated texts which, taken together, form a unitary whole. Each of the gospels was of course separately composed. Indeed not only does each of the Evangelists have his own quite distinctive literary style but each has a distinctive political and theological position. But all four gospels have formed a unity for the past 1700 years and it is a waste of time to try, at this late date, to unscramble the omelette. And anyway, if we could in fact achieve this impossible feat, the religious message which the texts contain would mostly be destroyed in the process. Each of the Evangelists tells his own story, but the gospel story that we all know is a blend of all four gospel stories and of other materials besides. And there is gain in such discrepancy. The Magi of Matthew 2.1 are not kings, and they are not three in number, and they do not offer their gifts to a Babe lying in a manger with an Ox and an Ass looking on and shepherds vaguely in the background. But, by blending Matthew 2.1 with Luke 2.1–19, and adding the classical tradition of the three gift-bearing Graces who should be the witnesses of every miraculous birth, we end up with a much better story.

In other words, I hold that the interesting part of the message which is embedded in the gospel texts is, as the texts themselves imply, a mystery which cannot be deciphered simply by looking at the superficial meaning of the individual stories. I agree that the New-Testament parables are not 'allegories' in the straightforward sense that seems to be asserted by the

Evangelists, but we deceive ourselves if we suppose that the parable mode of discourse and the allegorical mode of discourse are wholly distinct. Since I assume that all New-Testament texts (including parables) have a hidden (i.e. religious) meaning which is other than their manifest meaning, I am clearly unable to accept Nineham's view that stories which need to be deciphered should not be rated as parables!

In one form or another the difficulties posed by genre-distinction crop up in all branches of learning.

As knowledge accumulates, the sheer bulk of the available data leads to specialisation and this in turn leads to demarcation disputes and the over-elaboration of definitions. The two processes proceed in parallel. Within the general area with which we are now concerned, scholars who specialise in the study of myths distinguish themselves from those who concern themselves with folktales; folktale-experts are different from fairy-tale-experts. So myths, and folktales and fairy-tales must be given definitions which make the categories mutually exclusive. Before very long people begin to believe that the distinctions, which were probably introduced in the first place to satisfy some quirk of personal scholarly ambition, reflect 'real' discontinuities in the total field of data under review.

And that is what I am urging you to remember in the present case. It may be that there can be occasions when certain kinds of scholar will find it useful to distinguish 'parable' 'as a technical term' from all the other varieties of metaphorical, allegorical, analogical, fabulous, mimetic, proverbial, aphoristic, mythological, historical forms of story-text which crop up in the holy books of major religions, but there are certainly many other circumstances when the would-be decoder of a text will be well advised to forget about all such discriminations.

In what follows I shall be sticking to the rules. The only data which I shall consider in any detail will come from the New Testament. But, as you will see, I am taking the line that there is nothing special about 'parables' as such. All the stories which go to make up the Bible, both in the Old Testament and in the New, can be viewed in a parabolic mode; equally they can all be viewed as myth in the sense of 'sacred tale'.

Here of course I display the prejudices of an anthropologist. I do not share Professor Robson's dislike of 'myth' as an all purpose category of symbolic story.[2] But my point is that once a story of any kind becomes embedded in a text it is the text that concerns us. If we want to know what the text means we must consider the text as a whole not just the superficial content of particular segments of that text.

Just now I was attacking Professor Nineham's version of the orthodox Christian view that particular passages in the New Testament can be identified as transcriptions of what had once been the actual verbal utterances of an actual living preacher. Nevertheless, if we leave out Nineham's contentious reference to 'the circumstances of *utterance*', I certainly agree that the meaning of parables is 'essentially bound up with [their] original context'. The difference between us is that, by 'original context', I mean the directly discernible context of the New-Testament texts (as we now have them) together with a hypothetical social context in which these texts were put to use in the early Church at the time when the canon was first being established; whereas Nineham had in mind a much more imaginary context of a real Jesus, preaching from a real boat, to a real multitude, gathered on the real shore of the Sea of Galilee sometime around the year 30 A.D.

Perhaps it will help if I put this whole argument the other way round. If we concentrate only on the form and content of New-Testament parables, considered as individual stories, then there is nothing special about them. Considered simply as stories they are not distinguishable from Rabbinical parables, Jataka tales and so on. What makes them special is that they are Christian gospel stories which were used in early Christian rituals; it is in the rituals rather than the stories as such that we shall discover the mystery if there is any.

The phrase 'the structural study of', like the word 'parable', means different things to different people. For theological students it probably evokes the name of Rudolf Bultmann and the notion of 'form criticism'; anthropologists and literary men are more likely to assume a reference to the work of Lévi-Strauss or perhaps Roland Barthes. Folklore specialists will perhaps think of Vladimir Propp. These varied approaches to the study of the structure of literary texts share certain common ground, but this is certainly not an appropriate place to try to unravel their interconnections. In any case my own style of structural analysis makes no attempt to stick to anyone else's rules; it is not an orthodoxy, but no particular part of it is peculiar to myself.

Let us start then with the unchallengeable fact that the New Testament consists of a body of texts which have been used in Christian Church ceremonial ever since there was such a thing as an organised Christian Church. If we want to know what the Evangelists were getting at in their assertion that there are mysteries in the text – hidden meanings which are other than the superficial apparent meanings – then we need to pay close attention to this context of normal use.

For a social anthropologist there is nothing all that special about Christianity. At the most reductionist level all religious ceremonials are phenomena of the same kind; they are elements in a sequence of events which, considered as a whole, constitute a 'sacrifice', in the literal sense of 'a making sacred'.

Sacrifices, as ordinarily encountered by anthropologists, are procedures which involve the vicarious killing of an animal victim which 'stands for' the human donor of the sacrifice. The purpose of the sacrifice is to improve the ritual condition of the donor; the sinner achieves remission of sins, the sick are healed, the polluted are made clean. The way this benefit is brought about is that the procedures of the sacrifice establish a metaphysical bridge between the potent world of supernatural beings and the impotent world of humanity. Divine grace (*charisma*) flows through the sacrificial victim to the donor of the sacrifice.

Now obviously there are a great many religious rituals which are not 'sacrifices' in this crude prototype sense. Christians and Buddhists, Jains and Jews do not, in this day and age, kill animals as part of their ritual purification ceremonies. Nevertheless the Christians retain the ideology in its most extreme form; 'the full perfect and sufficient sacrifice for the remission of sins' is not just the killing of an animal but the killing of the man-god himself while the supreme sacrament of the Eucharist involves the symbolic eating of the body and blood of the divine victim.

We all know that, but what it is easy to forget is that the gospels were written after the event. As the story is told, the parables form part of the teaching of the living Jesus; as parables are used by the Church they form part of the teaching of the slain god and are mixed in with accounts of events in the life on Earth of that same slain god.

From a structuralist point of view the gospel story does not have a beginning and a middle and an end; it all exists in synchrony as in a dream. The beginning refers to the end, the end refers to the beginning. The total structure is metaphoric. The sequences in the story are simply a by-product of the nature of narrative. The text can only say one thing at a time but what it says next is very likely just the same as what it has said before but with the imagery twisted around.

The next point I want to make is not quite so straight forward. The nearest that most ordinary biblical scholars get to what I would myself recognise as a structural analysis is to search around in the text for the occurrence of a *chiasmus*, that is to say a sequence in which the elements run a:b:c:c:b:a. I do not understand just why this compositional form is felt to be especially interesting but the periodical *Semeia*, which tends to specialise in the structuralist analysis of biblical texts, is full of discussions of *chiasmus*, and John Fenton's Penguin commentary on St Matthew's gospel published in 1963 contains no less than twenty-two index-references to this somewhat way-out topic.

Anthropologists of my sort, for whom the study of ritual process seems at least as illuminating as the study of any body of text taken in isolation, have a somewhat comparable obsession with Van Gennep's theorising about *rites de passage*, which is also concerned with a kind of *chiasmus*.

According to Van Gennep (and the theory fits the facts surprisingly well) rituals which result in a change of ritual status of an initiate (and these of course include 'sacrifices' in the sense I have specified above) always have a tripartite structure: (i) 'a rite of separation', in which the initiate is separated from his/her original social role (ritual condition), is followed by (ii) a marginal state in which, temporarily, the initiate is outside society in a 'tabooed' condition which is ambivalently treated as dangerous-polluting or dangerous-holy. This is followed by (iii) 'a rite of aggregation' in which the initiate is brought back into society in his/her new social role (ritual condition). The logic of the exercise plainly implies that the symbolism involved in (i) should be more or less identical to that of (iii) but presented in reverse. For example if, as frequently happens, (i) the rite of separation includes a symbolic death and burial it is likely that (iii) the rite of aggregation will include a symbolic rebirth from the tomb (which has now become a womb symbol).

If, as anthropologists are inclined to argue, text and ritual sequence are directly equivalent then one might expect to find Van Gennep-style ritual sequences reflected in chiasmus-type verbal sequences. This must sound highly contrived and I would be the first to admit that Van Gennep-style analysis is so reductionist that, with a bit of ingenuity, it can be made to fit almost any empirical ritual sequence. But don't misunderstand me. I am not arguing that the Evangelists and their editors were consciously intending to make their texts function as a rubric for ritual performance but I am suggesting that the evidence from Dura-Europos strongly suggests that that is how segments of gospel text (story sequences) are likely to have been used by the early church.

If you accept that proposition then the potential conjunction of text and ritual action may well provide illumination. And this will be true whether we are discussing 'parables' as ordinarily understood or sections of text which have the form of historical narrative.

Anyway let us see where my version of the Van Gennep schema may fit in.

Just to show you what sort of connection between ritual and story we may expect to find, I will start with the passage about 'eagles' which, Professor Nineham tells us, was completely obscure even to the Evangelists, let alone anyone else.

The passage comes at Matthew 24.28 and is duplicated at Luke 17.37. In the King James version of Matthew the English text reads: 'wheresoever the carcase is, there will the eagles be gathered together'. The Revised Standard Version also has 'eagles' but includes 'vultures' as an alternative possibility. Later versions all have 'vultures'. A fairly typical commentary is that of Fenton (1963:388) who compares the passage to Job 39.30: 'This saying is probably proverbial, it means here that just as the vultures gather immediately a corpse appears, so the Son of Man will come to earth suddenly.' This is certainly the most obvious explanation even if the metaphor seems strange, because, both in Matthew and in Luke, the immediately preceding text refers to the cataclysmic events of the Second Coming and the Last Judgement. But there are other possibilities.

Both in Matthew and in Luke the emphasis is on the fact that while the multitude will perish the Elect will be saved. They will be saved by being where Christ is. But where will Christ be in this critical lightning flash of time? The passage about the 'eagles/vultures' is given in answer to *that* question. In Luke this is explicitly so: 'and they answered and said unto him, Where, Lord? And he said unto them, Wheresoever the body is, thither will the eagles be gathered together.'

Surely the body is the body of Christ and the eagles are the Elect gathered together at the Eucharist?

The Greek text of Matthew has *aetos* ('eagle'); the Hebrew of Job has *nesher*, which includes eagles, vultures and ospreys. Job's description corresponds to the 'griffon vulture' (*Gyps fulvus*). Like other vultures it lives off carrion, but even among fastidious Englishmen its spectacular flight has evoked rhapsodies of admiration rather than feelings of disgust. So if, as I claim, the allegorical reference in Matthew is to the Elect, then, although the 'vultures' of recent translations represents an improvement in ornithological accuracy, the traditional 'eagles' comes much closer to the original sense.

Perhaps you think this is a trivial point but it stands at the heart of our problem. Our difficulty is not just how to translate the original text, but how to understand the sense.

Please don't misunderstand me. I am not posing as a professional biblical scholar which most certainly I am not. It is simply that, if we consistently think of text in relation to ritual and *vice versa* instead of keeping the two modes of metaphorical expression in mutual isolation, then matters which might otherwise seem obscure may come into sharper or even quite different focus.

So with the Van Gennep triad in mind let us look at some larger chunks of gospel text.

Orthodox commentators have noted that in Matthew and Mark the story of the life of Jesus is punctuated by alternations between periods when the hero seems to lead a more or less normal life and periods when he is withdrawn to a place apart, which may be described as 'the wilderness' or 'a high mountain' or just a boat standing off-shore in the Sea of Galilee.

These commentators have further noted that the periods of withdrawal seem to precede manifestations of Jesus' divine power (e.g. Fenton (1963):242). I am not aware that any of these authors have suggested that there may be a transformational relationship between the discontinuities in the story and the discontinuities which crop up in a Van Gennep-type analysis of a *rite de passage*, yet if we assume such a parallelism the result can be illuminating.

Consider for example the miracles of the Feeding of the Five Thousand (Mark 6.32–44; Matthew 14.13–21; Luke 9.10–17; John 6.9–13) and the Feeding of the Four Thousand (Mark 8.1–9; Matthew 15.32–8). The former is one of the few miracles to be reported by all four Evangelists.

Orthodox modern commentators explain this last fact by noting that the early Christians found these stories especially important because they were held to contain a predictive cross-reference to the Eucharist. In making this observation these critics are of course conceding just the point I am trying to make, namely that there is a feedback relationship between the details of gospel text and the rituals in which they were used.

Indeed even those scholars who continue to assume that the gospel stories have a background of decipherable historical fact are now inclined to agree that all six stories must refer to the same event. But this latter conclusion then poses the additional problem of why both Mark and Matthew should tell the same story twice over. The suggested answers are diverse and elaborate and to my way of thinking wholly unconvincing.

So let us look at the several versions in context: Mark 6.32–44. [It will help you to follow my argument if you continuously cross-reference to Fig. 1]

Starting at the beginning of Chapter 6 we find Jesus in his own country where he is rejected and lacking in effective potency (v. 5). He sends off his disciples as travelling friars to preach and heal the sick.

101

They are to travel without worldly goods and to wear unusual and reduced clothing (v. 7–9). At v. 14–16 we learn that 'King Herod heard of him and he said that John the Baptist was risen from the dead.'

There is then a break in the continuity of the story which back-tracks to an account of the execution and burial of John the Baptist.

The disciples then return from their mission and, together with Jesus, withdraw by ship to a desert place. The crowds follow him. Jesus preaches to the multitude who are without food. The bread and fishes are miraculously provided. The form of the miracle (v. 41) is that of the Eucharist: 'he looked up to heaven, and blessed, and brake the loaves and gave them to his disciples to set before [the crowd]'. Jesus then sends his disciples back to the ship to cross over the water towards Bethsaida, but Jesus himself withdraws further into the mountains to pray.

A storm then arises and the ship is in difficulty. An epiphany then occurs in which Jesus appears walking on the sea. Jesus joins the disciples in the ship.

When they come to land it is in ordinary country, but Jesus is full of miraculous power: 'And whithersoever he entered, into villages, or cities, or country, they laid the sick in the streets and besought him that they might touch if it were but the border of his garment: and as many as touched him were made whole.'

In this case the *rite de passage* structure is very plain [Fig. 1]. Jesus and his disciples start as ordinary people in a domestic setting (A). Jesus has no special potency. The beginning of the 'rite of separation' concerns the disciples who are despatched as missionaries and told to wear special clothes and travel without the equipment of ordinary life (B).[3]

Then we have the references to John the Baptist: first Jesus is declared to be the replacement of John (C). Then the account of John's execution is predictive of the execution of Jesus (D). This is the sacrificial second phase of the 'rite of separation'. The third phase is the physical withdrawal of Jesus and the disciples in a boat across water to the wilderness (E). The crowd who follow are likewise moving from normality into a marginal condition of sanctity (F).

The miraculous feeding (where the loaves and fishes are surely to be understood as spiritual rather than material food) has the sacrificial form of the Eucharist proper (G). We are told of the crowd that they are as sheep to Jesus as shepherd (v.34), another detail of 'Paschal' imagery.

The beginning of the 'rite of aggregation' reverses section 3 of the 'rite of separation'; the disciples return across water to this world (H). But Jesus withdraws further into the Other World (I) before manifesting himself as divine (J). When he, in turn, returns to This World he has been transformed; he is full of divine *charisma* (K).

I hope you begin to see what I am getting at. I am not saying that the

I

OTHER WORLD

MARGINAL STATE (RITE DE MARGE)

A = Reference to Jesus' impotence in his home surroundings
B = Disciples sent out as friars in abnormal clothing
C = Reference to Jesus as John the Baptist replaced
D = Reference to execution of John (as sacrifice)
E = Withdrawal of Jesus and disciples to place apart
F = followed by Congregation of the faithful
G = Miraculous feeding of the Congregation (Eucharist)
H = Return of disciples to normality. (Reverse of E)
I = Withdrawal of Jesus to more remote place apart
J = Epiphany—Jesus revealed as divine person.
K = Jesus manifests divine power in normal surroundings

Figure 1. Rite of passage structure in relation to biblical feeding miracles.

story of the Feeding of the Five Thousand has the form of a parable 'in the narrow technical sense', but I am arguing that, when considered in context, it is parabolic.

The Feeding of the Five Thousand in the wilderness is palpably *like* the feeding of the Congregation at the Eucharist. Inversely I am suggesting that when we come to look at ordinary parables *in context* we should expect to find that they too have a 'religious' sense which depends upon their structural position in the overall narrative, and which is other than their more obvious sense. The contextualised version of Mark's account of the Feeding of the Five Thousand, which I have just given you, provides an example of such a contrast between ordinary narrative sense and religious sense.

But before we come around to parables proper let us take a look at the other versions of the miraculous feeding of the multitude.

The first Matthew sequence is identical to the first Mark sequence except that it omits the separate 'rite of separation' for the disciples. Thus in Matthew the equivalents to my indexed sections are:

A: 13.54–58. B: No equivalent. C: 14.1–2. D: 14.3–12.
E: 14.13a. F: 14.13b. G: 14.15–21. H: 14.22. I: 14.23.
J: 14.24–33. K: 14.34–6.

103

Luke's version [9.1–42] is significantly different. Most of my 'story units' are in the text but there is a change of key. There is no reference to Jesus' relative impotence in his homeland, as in Matthew 13.58, but earlier, at 8.19–21, Jesus has declared that he is already separated from his domestic upbringing: 'it was told him by certain which said that thy mother and thy brethren stand without, desiring to see thee. And he answered and said unto them, My mother and my brethren are these which hear the word of God and do it.' The whole of the rest of this chapter (8.22–34) is devoted to accounts of miraculous demonstrations of Jesus' power. But in this case also the sequence starts off with a 'rite of separation' (v. 22–5) in that Jesus and his disciples cross over water into a foreign land.

However Luke 9.1–6 corresponds to my '(B)' which was omitted by Matthew. So, in this version of the Feeding-Miracle, the stress is on the change of ritual status of the initiated disciples rather than on the transformation of Jesus from a human carpenter's son into a divine Messiah. This contrast corresponds to the fact that in Luke there is no reference to the baptism of Jesus by John. But there are then further differences:

> C/D: 9.7–9. E: 9.10 but in this case the withdrawal to the desert place does not entail the crossing of a water-barrier. F: 9.11. G: 9.12–17. But at this point, instead of sending the disciples back to the world of ordinary experience, Jesus initiates them into further mysteries. In place of the epiphany (J) of walking on the sea we have the epiphany of the Transfiguration in which Jesus is explicitly revealed as the Son of God to the three elect disciples, Peter, John and James. The locale for this revelation is a mountain (v. 28) remote from the ordinary world (I). Their return to normality is briefly reported (9.37): 'on the next day when they were come down from the hill, much people met him' (H). But Jesus then immediately manifests his supernatural power by healing a child possessed by an evil spirit (K).

John's Gospel comes closer to Mark and Matthew than to Luke but the differences are illuminating. The story comes at Chapter 6. There is no baseline reference to Jesus' own family, or to the initiation of the disciples as missionaries, or to the sacrificial execution of John. However at 5.32–8 Jesus makes the explicit claim that he is the divine replacement of the human John. So the initial sequence is:

> A: no reference. B: no reference. C: 5.32–8. D: no reference. E: 6.1. F: 6.2. But then at 6.4 we are told that the miraculous feeding takes place at the time of the Passover which reaffirms the symbolic link with the Eucharist by way of a cross-reference to the Last Supper and the Crucifixion. G: 6.5–14.

Then at 6.15 there is another innovation. 'When Jesus therefore perceived that they would come and take him by force, to make him a king, he departed again into a mountain himself alone.' The latter part of this sentence is my phase ('I') but the reference to kingship has not been encountered before. I will come back to that point in a moment. H: 6.17. J: 6.19.

But the '(K)' phase of the story, in which Jesus returns to This World, is very different. Where Mark has Jesus manifesting his supernatural powers by the performance of miracles, and makes the Epiphany a privilege of the Elite group of disciples on the ship, John (6.22–5), declares that the whole congregation was aware that Jesus had returned across the sea by miraculous means. But when they marvel at this Jesus says: 'Verily, verily, I say unto you, Ye seek me, not because ye saw the miracles, but because ye did eat the loaves, and were filled. Labour not for the meat which perisheth, but that meat which endureth unto ever-lasting life, which the Son of Man shall give unto you.' Vv. 28–58 then make it unambiguously clear that the 'true bread from heaven' which they have consumed is Jesus himself.

This pattern of a generalised 'near epiphany', accessible to all the faithful, corresponds to the fact that John provides no explicit account of the Transfiguration. Instead at 12.29–32, in a passage which is imme-diately predictive of the imminent Crucifixion, the general multitude hear the Voice of God give reassurance to a hesitant Jesus – another 'near epiphany'. In this immediate context v. 24 bears directly on what I shall say presently about the Parable of the Sower. It reads: 'except a corn of wheat fall into the ground and die, it abideth alone: but if it die, it bringeth forth much fruit'.

But to go back to John 6.15 and the reference to Kingship. This suggests a cross-reference to 12.12 where, in the sequence of narrative leading up to the Passion, we are told: '...much people that were come to the feast... took branches of palm trees ... and cried "Hosanna: blessed is the King of Israel that cometh in the name of the Lord."' But in context this is a transformation of a still later sequence:

A. 12.1. Jesus sups at the house of Lazarus whom Jesus had raised from the dead.
12.10. The chief priests consult whether they might put Lazarus to death
12.12–13. The multitude proclaim Jesus as King (as above).
B. 13.1 through to 17.26. John's account of The Last Supper which omits any specific reference to the Eucharist.
18.13–14, 24. The chief priests decide that Jesus shall be the sacrificial victim of whom 'it was expedient that one man should die for the people'
18.39–40. The multitude repudiate Jesus as King accepting Barabbas instead.

Further discussion of the ramifications of these transformations must be postponed until a later occasion[4].

But to go back to John's account of the Feeding-Miracle in Chapter 6, we may note that in the middle of the passage, where Jesus is speaking of himself as 'the living bread which came down from heaven', the sceptics intervene with (v. 42): 'Is not this Jesus, the son of Joseph, whose father and mother we know?' In terms of my diagram this serves to remind the reader/listener that, despite the metaphysics of the discourse, we are back in the real world of natural phenomena at '(K)'.

The accounts of the Feeding of the Four Thousand in Mark and in Matthew are almost identical, and I will not discuss them in detail. From my structuralist viewpoint it is obvious why Mark and Matthew should give the same story twice over. The 'feeding' is integral with the 'epiphany' – the earthly manifestation of Jesus as God. Luke and John have only one such scene, the Transfiguration in the one case, Jesus walking upon the water in the other; Mark and Matthew both give both epiphanies so they must both have two magical feedings. For the second epiphany the Van Gennep sequence is very imperfect, and this hardly seems surprising since the complete replication of the pattern would make the gospel narrative as a whole highly redundant.

So, where have we got to? Well at least I have shown that, if we postulate that a Van Gennep *rite-de-passage* structure underlies the variations of detail and sequence in the gospel stories of miraculous feeding, then the theory fits the evidence reasonably well. But I also claim to have said something significant about the religious 'message' contained in these texts. The structure that I have exhibited reinforces those elements in the text which explicitly affirm that, at the Day of Judgement (which will also be the ultimate Epiphany), the Saved will be those who stand close to Christ because they have participated in the Eucharist. Conversely it implies that, by participating in the Eucharist, the Faithful are ensuring that such an Epiphany will occur.

Whether you find this illuminating or trivial will depend upon your prior assumptions concerning the nature of the data. But what about parables?

My own argument, as I made clear earlier, is that there is no significant difference between sections of text which are ordinarily rated as parables and other sections which are considered by theologians to represent narrative history. From my point of view the stories about the miraculous feeding and its associated epiphany are as much 'parables' as any other. If these stories had been prefixed by some such phrase as: the mystery of the Eucharist is like ..., their parabolic nature would be generally recognised.

But that is not how things are, so I am now going to apply the same kind of analysis to a more prototypical set of parables. Insofar as there is consistent method in my madness, the crucial point to remember is that a section of text which appears to constitute a single 'story' must never be considered in isolation. Each section must be seen in relation to the surrounding text and also to other sections of text of broadly similar content.

But first, in view of the rather special nature of this audience, I must again lay stress on what I am *not* doing. I have some familiarity with the orthodox literature concerning parables which has been written in German and English over the past century. I do not pretend to any expertise in that field, but it is quite clear to me that the scholars in question start off with entirely different assumptions from myself. These assumptions are similar to those which I mentioned earlier when referring to Nineham. Very roughly they can be summarised as follows:

1. Jesus was a real person who existed in ordinary geographical space and ordinary historical time. He preached in Aramaic and he preached in parables.
2. The parables in our present gospel texts are for the most part fairly close reproductions of what Jesus actually said.
3. They derive, either directly or by devious indirect routes, from an entirely hypothetical source written in Aramaic. This hypothetical source is presumed to have been written by an author with an encyclopaedic facsimile memory, quite soon after the events it purported to record.
4. But although, as a consequence of this hypothetical literary activity, the gospel parables correspond closely to what Jesus actually said, the commentaries and explanations of the parables which are also part of our present text, represent later accretions derived from theological prejudices prevalent in 'the early Church'. Scholars who today find themselves out of sympathy with these early Christian tendencies, which include, for example, an incipient antisemitism, feel themselves free to reject the whole of the, supposedly inauthentic, supplementary material.
5. Modern commentaries on the parables thus consist in large measure of assertions about what Jesus 'really meant' by what he 'really said'. There is no consensus. The only thing that the scholars seem to be agreed about is that the real Jesus cannot possibly have meant what the text says he meant.

My own starting-point is entirely different. I do not believe that Jesus was an historical personage at all. For me he has the dramatic, mythical, poetical reality of Sophocles' Oedipus. Moreover, even if there was a Jewish carpenter's son who became a prophet around the time of Josephus, we cannot hope to know anything about him.

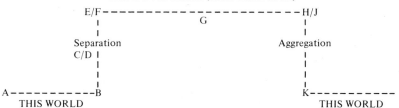

I

OTHER WORLD

MARGINAL STATE (RITE DE MARGE)

E/F – H/J
     | G |

Separation   Aggregation
C/D |

A – – – – – – – – – –B   K– – – – – – – – – –
   THIS WORLD   THIS WORLD

A–B = Jesus separates himself from his family: (Matthew)
C = Reference to Jesus as John the Baptist replaced
D = Reference to execution of John (as sacrifice)
E = Withdrawal of Jesus and disciples to place apart [a ship]
G = Jesus addresses the multitude in parables
H = Return to normality. (Reverse of E)
I = Withdrawal to more remote place apart
      [(a) a house: (b) country of the Gadarenes]
J = Epiphany—Jesus revealed as divine [to the maniac]
K = Jesus manifests divine power in normal surroundings
      [raising of Jairus' daughter etc.]

Figure 2. Rite of passage structure in relation to the Parable of the Sower.

The gospels tell us no more about the living Jesus (if there was one) than the plays of Shakespeare tell us about the living Shakespeare. It is absurd to imagine that we can evade this deficiency by inventing additional gospels which correspond to none of the texts that we now have. Of course I realise that our present gospel-texts must certainly derive from earlier texts which have now disappeared, but there are no grounds for supposing that if we possessed these lost scriptures we would know any more about the historical Jesus than we do now.

Shakespeare's sources for *Hamlet* are no closer to 'history' than *Hamlet* itself; and anyway we do not read *Hamlet* in order to learn about the history of Denmark or Sophocles to learn about the history of Athens or Thebes.

So whatever there is to be discovered about biblical parables is already there in the text. It cannot be conjured out of the imaginations of theologians however learned they may be.

That said, let us take a look at the Parable of the Sower as recounted by Matthew keeping in mind the *rite de passage* structure that we used before [Fig. 2]

A/B: We start at Matthew 12.46–50 with Jesus asserting his separation from his own family. This is Matthew's version of Luke 8.19–21 which, as

108

we have seen, serves the same 'rite of separation' function prior to Luke's version of the feeding miracle.

C/D: no explicit equivalent. E. 13.1–2. Jesus moves from the shore into a ship standing off-shore and addresses the multitude from the ship leaving a strip of water in between.

G. 13.3–52. This section contains a long series of parables most of which are addressed to the multitude (presumably from the ship). But there are sub-sections [vv. 10–23; vv. 36–52] which contain explanations of parables and also additional parables which are addressed to the disciples alone. Indeed at v. 36 Jesus sends the multitude away and, together with the disciples, withdraws further 'into the house' (phase 'I' of the diagram). J. There is no explicit epiphany.

H/K: (reversal of E) 13.53–4. Jesus returns to his own country and his own family and a state of relative impotence (this is where my analysis of the feeding-miracles started out).

The structuralist argument then is that this whole sequence is a kind of preliminary 'dry run' for the Eucharist/Epiphany sequence. In that case the parables and their interpretations (G/I) ought to be equivalent in some sense to the story about the feeding of the multitude with the mystical body of Christ himself. And this is just what the text in fact says.

I have already given you the crucial link which is the passage in John 12.23–9 where, in the immediate context of the semi-epiphany in which the multitude hear the Voice of God, Jesus predicts his own death using the simile of sown wheat:

> Except a corn of wheat fall into the ground and die, it abideth alone: but if it die it bringeth forth much fruit.

The immediate equivalents in the synoptic gospel versions of the Parable of the Sower have the same implication but leave out the direct reference to death. In Matthew the most immediate equivalents are:

> 13.4 And when he sowed, some seeds fell by the way side, and the fowls came and devoured them up ...

> 13.8 But other fell into good ground, and brought forth fruit, some an hundredfold, some sixtyfold, some thirtyfold.

In the text, in the passages where Jesus explains the various parables to the disciples, the references are to hearing and seeing but failing to understand. But what is 'the word of the Kingdom' that is not understood? The orthodox commentators seem to me to be extraordinarily insensitive to this quite central issue. Surely this crucial phrase, in this context especially, simply *must* refer to the central dogma of the Church, namely that Christ died for our redemption and that the bread and wine of the Eucharist is the mystical body of Christ sacrificed. If this *is* the code then the whole set of parables in Matthew 13 along with the interpretations provided for the disciples fall into place.

My time has run out so you must work out the details for yourselves; but if, all the way through the chapter, you substitute the expression 'the manifestation of Christ/Jesus in the Eucharist' for the text expressions which in King James Version appear as: 'the mysteries of the kingdom of heaven', 'the word of the kingdom', 'the word', 'the kingdom of heaven', then you will find that everything falls into place without leaving any residual puzzles at all.

The only reason that ordinary commentary does not accept this view is that the orthodox scholars are so literal-minded. When Jesus was preaching in Galilee he was still alive, and the Eucharist was not yet invented; so how can the Miracle of the Feeding of the Multitudes, let alone the parables of the sown seed, have originally referred to the death and resurrection of Christ made manifest through the Eucharist?

If such scholars would only recognise that the time of the gospel stories is mythical time, in which no one event happens before or after any other event, then all the puzzles disappear, or at any rate all the puzzles that the orthodox commentators seem to find especially worrying about these particular bodies of text.

The same analysis will fit the corresponding text in Mark 3.31–5.43. But in this case not only are there fewer parables but after their completion at 4.34 the H/K section is expanded. Jesus makes several journeys by sea and performs a variety of miracles. Moreover at Mark 5.6, when he is 'on the other side of the sea ... in the mountains and in the tombs' (I), he encounters a maniac who recognises him as the 'Son of the most high God' (J). There then follow a sequence of especially impressive miracles which include first: the Miracle of the Gadarene Swine which occurs in the foreign country of the Gadarenes. Here the spirits by which the maniac is possessed are transferred to a herd of swine. Then, after a further voyage by sea (H), Jesus' new potency after his return from the Other World of the dead is emphasised by the healing of the woman with an issue of blood (5.25–34) (an appropriate symbolic cross-reference to the restoration of fertility to the infertile), and then by the equally appropriate miracle of the restoration of life to Jairus' dead daughter.

Thus the sequence I/J/H/K, which is given low emphasis in Matthew, is stressed very strongly by Mark.

Luke's version is different again but closer to Mark than to Matthew:

A/B. No equivalents.
C. 7.17–35. A long passage emphasising that Jesus is a superior replacement of John but omitting any reference to John's death.
D. No direct equivalent.

E. (withdrawal). At 7.36–50 Luke has the scene in which Jesus dines with a Pharisee named Simon and the repentant prostitute (Mary Magdalene by later tradition) anoints Jesus' feet with myrrh.

G. 8.4–18. The Parable of the Sower is given to a large congregation. The usual 'explanation' of the parable is given to the disciples, the seed here being described as 'the word of God'.

Luke's supper scene is not explicitly associated with the Passover, but the stories in John (12.3) and Matthew (26.7) which do have such an explicit association are very similar. Certainly if the text of John is taken into account Luke's Parable of the Sower is not far removed from the bread of the first Eucharist. Luke's Parable of the Sower is followed by the Parable of the Candle: 'No man when he hath lighted a candle, covereth it with a vessel, or putteth it under a bed; but setteth it on a candlestick, that they which enter may see the light.' And this brings us back again to 8.19–21 with its reference to Jesus' mother and his brethren (K). But at this point the E/K part of the cycle starts again:

E (ii). 8.22 Jesus withdraws by boat across the sea. He calms a storm. On the other side, in the country of the Gadarenes, he encounters the maniac from the tombs ... The sequence I/J/H/K continues as in Mark Chapter 5.

This last sequence, as can be seen, provides a most explicit reference to the various epiphanies that are destined to occur after Jesus' death and resurrection from the tomb. By implication, the Parable of the Sower refers to that which leads up to that crisis, i.e. the Last Supper and the institution of the Eucharist.

The odd thing is that in the early history of Christianity most of the interpretations which I have been imposing on the data by use of my structuralist diagram were accepted as entirely orthodox doctrine. It was taken for granted that the whole of human history is 'predictive' of divinely ordained human destiny. Events that were supposed to have happened in the past are primarily of interest because of what they might tell us about the future. No one thought of historical time as we do before the sixteenth Century.

It was only in relatively recent times, since history and myth came to be distinguished, that the pedants have tried to impose less straightforward, less poetic, interpretations on the metaphors of the gospel texts. Somehow the candlesticks have got mixed up.

My own very simplistic view is that the early Christians, and by that I mean the Christians of the second and third Centuries A.D., who most certainly did not think about time in this modern way, probably knew

111

a good deal more about the meaning of the gospel texts than do the present-day inheritors of German nineteenth-Century Higher Criticism.

Notes

1 Dr Michael Goulder's contribution to the Seminar indicated that Nineham has here oversimplified the facts.
2 Professor Wallace Robson's contribution to the seminar discussed, among other things, the use of several of the genre categories to which I am objecting.
3 In discussion Dr Goulder appeared to question whether Jesus' instructions to his disciples could bear this 'rite of separation' interpretation. I find this surprising. The text reads: 'And he called unto him the twelve, and began to send them forth two by two; and gave them power over unclean spirits; and commanded them that they should take nothing for their journey, save a staff only; no scrip, no bread, no money in their purse: but be shod with sandals; and not put on two coats' (Mark 6.7–9).
4 In my lecture as delivered, I purposely omitted any reference to the mention of 'kingship' at John 6.15. I thereby earned a rebuke from Bishop Montefiore, who seemed to think I was cheating! In fact my omission was simply a space-saver. The cross-reference passage in John Chapter 18 was the subject of a celebrated discursus by Sir James Frazer in *The Golden Bough* (3rd Edition: Part VI: 'The Scapegoat': pp. 412–23). My Frazer Lecture, 'Kingship and Divinity', given in Oxford in October 1982 was devoted to a reconsideration of the various strands of circumstantial evidence concerning the ritual aspects of the Crucifixion of Christ, to which Frazer there drew our attention.

References

Fenton, J. C. 1963 *The Gospel of Saint Matthew*, The Pelican New Testament Commentaries, Harmondsworth: Pelican Books

Finney, P. C. 1977 'Antecedents of Byzantine Iconoclasm: Christian Evidence before Constantine', in J. Gutmann (ed.) *The Image and the Word: Confrontations in Judaism, Christianity and Islam* pp. 27–48, Missoula (Montana): Scholars Press

Frazer, J. G. 1911–15, 1936 *The Golden Bough*, 3rd Edition, 13 Volumes, London: Macmillan

Gutmann, J. 1973 'Programmatic Painting in the Dura Synagogue', in J. Gutmann (ed.) *The Dura-Europos Synagogue* pp. 137–54, Missoula (Montana): American Academy of Religion/Society of Biblical Literature

Nineham, D. E. 1963 *The Gospel of Saint Mark*, The Pelican New Testament Commentaries, Harmondsworth: Pelican Books.

6 The fate of Lot's wife: structural mediation in Biblical mythology

D. ALAN AYCOCK

A theme recurrent in mythology is the immoblization of a hero or villain, together with his/her transformation into an inanimate object.[1] To my knowledge, however, Lévi-Strauss is the first to have offered a satisfactory explanation of this immobilization/transformation theme, in his analysis of the Tsimshian 'Asdiwal' cycle: the hunter Asdiwal's transmutation into stone comes as the final result of a complex series of symmetrical geographic, social, economic, and cosmological oppositions expressed in the myth and developed through a dialectic, in which the actions of Asdiwal himself represent the dynamic mediation of thesis and antithesis (1967: 1–47). Even Mary Douglas, who is by no means uncritical of Lévi-Strauss, is obliged to remark of his analysis that: 'Some may have doubted that myths can have an elaborate symmetrical structure. If so, they should be convinced of their error' (1967: 56).

To interpret an instance of immobilization and transformation, therefore, it seems that we must invoke the wider symbolic structure of the myth, insofar as that structure expresses contradictory events or tendencies. We must then inquire whether the character who becomes immobilized and changed embodies a midpoint between these contradictions, in such a way that the mythic plot cannot further unfold unless this dramatic resolution occurs.[2]

My purpose in this paper is to argue that the 'recipe' I have outlined in the above paragraph is entirely adequate to enable us to understand what must otherwise remain a mysterious mythological event, namely, the transformation of Lot's wife into a pillar of salt. Lest the attainment of this goal be viewed as more trivial than triumphant, I hasten to add that I perceive the myth of Lot to be a structural analogue of many other, more significant myths in the Old and New Testaments, and that I expect my unravelling of the fate of Lot's wife, together with an explication of the accompanying symbolic structure, to suggest interesting resonations throughout Hebraic and Christian mythology.

In view, however, of Professor Julian Pitt-Rivers' recent (1977) critique

113

of 'structuralist' Biblical exegeses, I wish to enter three *caveats* at this point. First, although I regard this essay as inspired by the work of Claude Lévi-Strauss (as well as by that of Sir Edmund Leach), I am not claiming either to be acting within any theoretical parameters he may have set out, or to be producing an analysis that Lévi-Strauss himself might identify as 'structural'. What I have written here ought to be judged on its own merits and limitations. Second, I am not proposing that this analysis unravels the *only* message to be discovered in the myth of Lot and his wife; it is entirely possible that there might be as many exegetically valid messages as there are persons inclined towards hermeneutics. My only canon of success is to generate an interpretation which, among others, may be regarded as intellectually and aesthetically satisfying by myself and at least some of my readers. Third, I do not accept Pitt-Rivers' prohibition upon the structural analysis of any text falling toward the consciously prescriptive end of his continuum between myth and 'real' history (1977: 140ff.). I think that the 'irreversibility' and 'progression' of moral history is another part of its message(s), not a factor somehow extrinsic to the text itself, and therefore subject to the same approach as any other part of the text. I have correspondingly incorporated that factor into my analysis.

I shall not recount the myth of Lot, since it is readily available to any reader not familiar with its details.[3] In studying the myth, I was immediately struck by a series of contradictory events which 'bracket' the changing of Lot's wife into a pillar of salt.

First, the myth begins with a recounting of the hospitality offered by Lot to the two angels in disguise sent by God to inform him of the extent of iniquity in Sodom. The hospitality, prescribed by the *mores* of ancient (as well as modern) Semitic-speaking peoples, consisted of a feast together with unleavened bread.[4] The end of the myth, on the other hand, tells of the drunkenness of Lot as a consequence of the wine given him by his daughters. Thus a sequence which commences with restraint and social formality concludes with intemperance and social insensibility.

A second theme closely related to the first involves the identities of Lot's companions. At the beginning of the myth, these companions are two males,[5] disguised, and strangers to Lot. At the ending of the myth, the companions are two females, 'disguised' by Lot's drunkenness, and his intimates in more than one sense.

Third, the myth starts with the impending destruction of Sodom by God, but ends with the creation of the tribes of the Moabites and Ammonites, descended from the incestuous relationship of Lot with his daughter.

114

Fourth, the myth is initially located within the city walls of Sodom, and ultimately set in a cave in the hills above Zoar. This geographical movement might best be understood as a contrast of the 'Culture' of the city with the 'Nature' of the wilderness, an opposition familiar to students of Lévi-Strauss (1969) and Sir Edmund Leach (1976).

Finally, the myth begins in a society of homosexuals, who by virtue of their (apparently exclusive) sexual preference *cannot* produce children (we may also note the symbolic blinding/castration of the men of Sodom by the angels in disguise). The myth ends in an incestuous association precipitated by Lot's daughters, who justify their actions by asserting that they *must* bear children (the womb-like locale of this event, in the caves in the hills above Zoar, is most appropriate).

Turning now to the problem of mediation, how is it that the miraculous transformation of Lot's wife into a pillar of salt 'resolves' the contradictions posed above?

The key to my argument is that Lot's wife became, specifically, a pillar of *salt*: this particular fate may be interpreted most clearly in the context of the ethnography of the ancient Mediterranean. Salt, to the ancient Hebrews, had three main connotations: first, it was a symbol of purification, preservation, and immortality; second, it was a symbol of barrenness and sterility; third, it was a symbol of covenant, as between parties concluding a peace treaty or a marriage agreement (Gaster 1969: 301–2, 428–30, 516–17, 618–19; Smith 1927: 270, 454). All three of these meanings are relevant to my demonstration (I consider the actual presence of considerable quantities of salt in the geographical region indicated by the myth neither to substantiate nor to vitiate the explanations offered here).

Let us consider, first, salt in relation to the social control implied by Lot's hospitality to the disguised angels, and in relation to the social excess implied by Lot's drunkenness. A well-known Semitic metaphor equates hospitality with salt shared betwen guest and host; indeed, every instance of commensality, *including* sacrifices offered to God, is to be accompanied by appropriate seasoning with salt (Gaster 1969 and Smith 1927; *loc. cit.*). In effect, I suppose we could say that the fate of Lot's wife is an extraordinary affirmation of sociability: she has been offered up as a sacrifice to God in much the same way Lot offered food to the disguised angels, and offered his daughters to the men of Sodom,[6] as testimony to his hypertrophied sense of *politesse*. In contrast, we might point to the lack of social control instanced by Lot's drunkenness, and equate this with the disobedience of his wife, with its saline consequence. More to the point, I think, are the divine interventions which constitute a direct response to the instances of social control and social excess: the disguised angels miraculously deliver Lot and his family from Sodom and its inhabitants as a reward for his hospitality; God, accepting Lot's 'sacrificial' offering, simultaneously punishes Lot's wife for her excessive attachment to a doomed city; Lot's 'sacred' drunkenness (Dumézil 1973: 21ff. has much to say on this subject in Norse and Indic contexts) spares him culpability for his incest, which itself was linked to the imagery of divinity and elitism in the ancient Near East. Salt is important here, therefore, to evoke the idea of mediation between God and man.

The contrast between the identities of Lot's guests and those of his daughters is precisely resolved by Lot's wife. The plot logically requires a means of transition from Lot's interaction with the two angels to Lot's interaction with his two daughters. His wife provides such a transition, or mediation, since she embodies qualities of both daughters and angels: like his daughters, Lot's wife is an intimate and a member of his household, but unlike most characterizations in Pentateuchal mythology, Lot's wife is never named, nor is she genealogically attached to one of the patriarchs. In this latter respect, therefore, she is more like the strangers who prove to be angels; indeed, we might even say that Lot's wife attains an apotheosis in her fate which is not unlike that of other figures of the mythology of classical antiquity.

The contradiction between the destruction of Sodom and the creation of the Moabites and Ammonites, which arises from the structure of the myth, leads us again to the imagery of salt which the fate of Lot's wife presents: both the discontinuity implied by the obliteration of the cities of Sodom and Gomorrah, and the continuity implied by the divine blessing required for the creation of new social groups, are subsumed for the ancient Hebrews by the idea of covenants attested through the sharing of salt. We may say that on the one hand a covenant implies discontinuity: since it entails mutual obligations newly recognized by the parties, these obligations must not have previously existed (as in a marriage contract or a peace treaty). On the other hand, a covenant required the *imprimatur* of ancestral approval ultimately derived from God's authority, and here the continuity involved in the creation of any social form must be acknowledged. Thus, the metamorphosis of Lot's wife embodies a covenant between God and Lot which must formally be accompanied by a communion of salt. Salt, of course, may also here be viewed as symbolic of the preservation of the covenant.

I think, then, that we ought to accept the geographical journey of Lot and his family from Sodom to the hills above Zoar as a metaphoric rite of passage from an old society to a new one. Here it is tempting to refer to the symbolic immobilizations which many cultures impose to emphasize the non-social character of persons undertaking the liminal phase of a rite of passage (Turner 1967: 93–111). The permanent geographical immobilization of Lot's wife in the wilderness of Nature between the old Culture of Sodom and the new Culture emanating from the caves in the hills above Zoar should thus be interpreted as a moral analogy of her permanently liminal status in the rite of passage she chose to abort. Here again, the preservative function of salt was employed during rites of passage by the ancient Hebrews in an attempt to safeguard the purity and permanence of the status about to be entered upon (see references already cited in Gaster 1969).

We may go further than this, and argue that Lot's wife, by virtue of her statuses of wife and mother, is anomalous both in the society of homosexuals she has abandoned, and in the incestuous ménage à trois which eventuates. Her mediating position, therefore, must be one of immobilization, since she would be in a contradictory situation were she to go either forward or back. Perhaps the barrenness of salt is a uniquely suitable image for Lot's wife as wife or mother in either society, since her reproductive functions are irrelevant to both.

Finally, the statuses of Lot's wife as woman and as a genealogical 'stranger' also doom her to immobility between the initial and final events of the myth. If we study the 'abominations' of Leviticus, it is clear that rules about food and rules about sexuality are equated by the ancient Hebrews, as by so many other peoples. In particular, the rules stress the 'separateness' of interaction in both cases, and assign a 'clean' or 'pure' condition to those who conscientiously observe the rules which separate various kinds of foods on the one hand, and various kinds of sexual partners on the other (Douglas 1966). Both intercourse with a person of one's own sex and intercourse with a person of one's own kin group are therefore 'abominable' and 'unclean'. Lot's wife, as a *female*, is thus anomalous in Sodomite society: as a member (presumably) of a kin group *separate* from Lot's own, she is anomalous also in his incestuous relationship with his daughters. It may be supposed that the salt into which she is transformed has therefore not only the connotation of sterility, but also the connotation of purity, since she cannot, by definition, participate in the abominations and impurity of either Sodom or the caves in the hills.

I shall now suppose, however presumptuously, that I have established both the symmetry and the contradictions in the myth of Lot, and further that I have shown that the fate of Lot's wife is appropriate and necessary to her role as mediator of these contradictions. As I have already suggested, this exercise would be of limited value if it had no further application. However, even a modest inquiry assures us of the proliferation of immobilized or suspended heroes in Biblical mythology: Noah in his ark upon Ararat, Isaac tied to the altar below Abraham's knife and the ram caught in the bushes who substitutes for him, and Jesus on the cross are some prominent examples. Furthermore, the oppositions I have elicited from this myth are likewise standard themes: excess and restraint applied to food and sexuality, the city and the wilderness, the ambiguous status of women in a formally patrilineal society and the relation of covenant to sacrifice are ideas which inform key metaphors throughout the Old and New Testaments.

Notes

1 For other examples of immobilization/transformation, see the examples and bibliography cited in Gaster 1969: 160–1, 366 (n. 1).
2 Although the transformation of Asdiwal is the conclusion of that specific story in the cycle, Lévi-Strauss argues in effect that its sequel, which concerns Waux, the son of Asdiwal, cannot be justified without that particular dénouement (1967: 23ff.).
3 All references in this essay to the myth of Lot are taken from Gen. 19: 1–38, in the Revised Standard Edition of the Christian Bible.
4 This specification of the offering of unleavened (and unsalted) bread seems significant in the light of subsequent events. Perhaps I ought to suggest a contrast between the *unsalted* bread at the beginning of the myth, and the wine (which in ancient times would have been made *with* salt) at its ending?
5 The 'twoness' of the angels is part of the Old Testament manifestation of divinity, regarded there as a plural noun.
6 A confrontation of purity with abomination which is both dramatically satisfying, and, as later events prove, entirely ironic. I am indebted to Dr Brent Shaw for pointing out to me this facet of the myth.

References

Douglas, Mary 1966 *Purity and Danger; an Analysis of Concepts of Pollution and Taboo*, London: Routledge and Kegan Paul
    1967 'The meaning of myth, with special reference to "La Geste d'Asdiwal"', in Edmund Leach (ed.), *The Structural Study of Myth and Totemism*, London: Tavistock Publications Ltd
Dumézil, Georges 1973 *Gods of the Ancient Northmen* (E. Haugen, ed. and trans.), Berkeley: University of California Press
Gaster, Theodor H. 1969 *Myth, Legend, and Custom in the Old Testament* (2 vols.), New York: Harper and Row
Leach, Edmund 1976 *Culture and Communication: the Logic by Which Symbols are Connected*. Cambridge: Cambridge University Press.
Lévi-Strauss, Claude 1967 'The story of Asdiwal' (N. Mann, trans.), in Edmund Leach (ed.), *The Structural Study of Myth and Totemism*, London: Tavistock Publications Ltd.

1969 *The raw and the cooked; introduction to a science of mythology* (J. and D. Weightman, trans.), New York: Harper and Row

Pitt-Rivers, Julian 1977 'The Fate of Shechem or the Politics of Sex,' in Pitt-Rivers, *The Fate of Shechem or the Politics of Sex: Essays in the Anthropology of the Mediterranean*, Cambridge: Cambridge University Press.

Smith, W. Robertson 1889 *Lectures on the Religion of the Semites*, 1st Edition (London: A. & C. Black), 2nd Edition 1894. 3rd Edition (edited by S. A. Cook) 1927

Turner, Victor 1967 'Betwixt and between: the liminal period in *rites de passage*', in *The Forest of Symbols*, Ithaca, New York: Cornell University Press

7 The Mark of Cain

D. ALAN AYCOCK[1]

Although conclusions about structuralism's respectability have been somewhat obfuscated by the fervent disputations of the past two decades, both apostles and apostates seem to agree that a structural exegesis produces results which would not have been accessible to a 'common-sense' perspective alone. This claim may cut two ways, of course, but I prefer to regard it as fulfilling a canon both of scientific and artistic credibility (cf. Geertz 1966).

For example, I think that a lay Christian would be hard-pressed to think of any figures in Christian mythology more antithetical than Cain and Jesus, yet we can very quickly satisfy ourselves (as I shall attempt to demonstrate) that these two 'heroes' are precise structural analogues of one another. Such a conclusion is not particularly enlightening from the point of view of the everyday moralist (indeed, it might be exceptionally threatening), but it is both scientifically useful and aesthetically pleasing to the mythologist to make such a comparison.[2]

Given no more elaborate an *apologia* than this, let us consider one context in which Jesus and Cain are comparable. I refer specifically to stigmata. The stigmata of Jesus have been celebrated throughout Christian history, displayed by ecstatic disciplines as evidence of unusual piety. The stigma of Cain is no less attested by scripture (Gen. 4.15),[3] though the disciples of Cain (with the possible exception of Lady Macbeth) are less eager to exhibit the mark of their allegiance.

How are we to understand the stigmata of Jesus and Cain? A metaphor is a rhetorical device which links the visible to the moral at several levels of awareness (Turner 1967, 1970, 1974); stigmata may therefore be regarded metaphorically, as visual clues to the moral status of a particular actor, where it is important that the moral status of that actor be *multivalent*, according to the level of interpretation which the audience invokes. This multivalence is diagnostic of mythologic contexts, producing in the audience an intuition simultaneously of emotional involvement and of interpretive complexity (Cohen 1969).

In the myths of Cain and Jesus there are four distinguishable, but interrelated, levels subsumed by the metaphor of stigma: (1) stigma as an existential paradox expressing contradiction between physical mortality and spiritual immortality; (2) stigma as a sort of brand, a mark of 'ownership' by a particular deity who sets apart the stigmatized person from his society and thus from conventional morality; (3) stigma as an element of sacrifice, mediating the realms of the human and the divine; (4) stigma as a mythic paradox of creation and destruction akin to the worldwide theme of the 'trickster'. I will consider these points in the order given above.

1. Stigma as an existential paradox

Both E. B. Tylor and Ernest Becker perceived that life and death generate a fundamental contradiction of human experience: for Tylor (1958), this contradiction arose from sleep and dreaming, and led to a soul-hypothesis; for Becker (1973), the contradiction was directly existential, and was expressed in human cultures as an opposition between social control and physical vulnerability, purity and pollution, and Culture and Nature. Nevertheless, both scholars emphasized the transmutation of a cognitive dilemma into a paradox of thought *and* action; neither denied that a model of cultural behavior might be psychogenic in origin.

A stigma may be regarded as a metaphor which embodies this contradiction of the physical and the spiritual. For example, the gospel of John (20.19–31) emphasizes that the wounds in Jesus' hands, feet, and side are not merely the stigmata of mortality which they superficially resemble, but the visible evidence of spiritual immortality which redeems (purifies) the community of believers. This paradox of physical mortality and spiritual immortality is illumined dramatically by the resurrection scene of all four gospels: although women are present (as at an ordinary physical birth), it is made clear that they do not participate, to distinguish the spiritual immortality of Jesus, ancestor of the 'new covenant', from the contaminating circumstances of normal birth as provided in Levitical doctrine (Lev. 12).

Similarly, although God places upon Cain's forehead a stigma, a physical blemish denoting Cain as uniquely associated in human history with murder, God has designated Cain in this way precisely in order that *no one shall kill him* (Gen. 4.15). This metaphor of the paradox of physical mortality and spiritual immortality is precursor to an even greater evidence of Cain's role as culture-hero: he becomes ancestor both of city-dwellers and of those who live in tents and herd cattle, while his descendants introduce to human society both arts and industry (Gen. 4.17–22). Thus from Cain's violent act of mortality arise exactly those activities which typify Culture, in its immortal sense.

2. Stigma as a mark of ownership

From a slightly different perspective, stigmata consecrate by a mark of divine 'ownership' much as priestly vestments cause a cleric to stand out from the laity as 'constructively in attendance upon the person of the divinity whose livery he wears' (Veblen 1953: 128).[4] Cain's consecration is effectively demonstrated by God's threat to retaliate 'sevenfold' (Gen. 4.15), against anyone attempting to exact blood-vengeance for Cain's murder of Abel. Similarly, a central theme of the New Testament is the oft-iterated assertion of Jesus' unique status as Son of God, the focal relationship of a patrilineal society.

The effect of consecration is to remove an individual from his moral community: 'the person with a stigma is not quite human' (Goffman 1963: 5). Thus, Cain is not to be slain although he is a murderer, and Jesus rejects by verbal and physical abuse the authority and property-structure of Palestinian society.

This characterization of the stigmatized as anti-social is thematically essential, to permit them, as mediators neither human nor divine, to communicate in both realms. Furthermore, it emphasizes the creativity generated by release from stereotypic social roles and norms. Both mediation and creativity are, as we shall see, explicit in the ritual of sacrifice.

3. Stigma as an element of sacrifice

The extensive catalogues of Hebrew 'abominations' found in Leviticus and Deuteronomy clearly argue the importance to early Judaism of the separation and opposition of social and physical aspects of experience: the cultural classification of 'clean' species and appropriate social behavior is specifically threatened by 'polluting' species and behavioral improprieties which present classificatory anomalies at the *margins* of the social order (Douglas 1966; see also Soler 1979). Yet 'dirt' is not only dangerous; it is also powerful and creative, since it is not circumscribed by the conceptual order of society. Both purity and pollution are therefore essential complements in any ritual process (Turner 1969).

In this context, sacrifice can be regarded as the Hebrew ritual activity *par excellence* (Leach 1976: 81–93). Consider the basic structure of Hebrew sacrifice and in particular the way it incorporates and integrates basic oppositions to achieve both 'structure' and 'anti-structure' in social process. To use the terminology of Hubert and Mauss (1964), the human *sacrifier* (as sponsor) establishes a temporary identification with the animal victim, which is itself conceptually divided into two parts, clean and polluted. The victim is slaughtered by the sacrificer, an elaborately purified representative of society, and the polluted (or stigmatizing) parts – blood and fat, as well as the organs which contain or are surrounded by blood and fat – burnt in deference to their threatening power of natural creativity and mortality, while the clean parts are devoured as a symbolic incorporation of cultural structure, pure and immortal (see also Turner 1977 for a discussion of sacrifice in a yet more abstract philosophical framework).

Note that the act of identification with the victim, however transitory, is nevertheless fraught with a creative fertility so potent and dangerous that all participants must be continuously protected and decontaminated by numerous ritual cleansings and separations (taboos) prior to, during, and subsequent to the sacrifice itself. The sacrificer (usually a priest), moreover, is permanently held separate from the everyday life of his community to facilitate communication between the human and the supernatural, without risk to the former. Part of the rite of priestly consecration, appropriately, requires a stigmatization of the initiate by the polluted, yet fertile, blood of a sacrificial victim (Lev. 8.23ff.).[5]

Stigmata, prominent during the most potent moments of the ritual, express the contrasts between the important conceptual elements of sacrifice – purity and pollution, human and animal, life and death, limitation and creativity, this world and the other world – in such a way that the stigmatized may be perceived as inhabiting permanently the interface (or margin) of these oppositions. As predicted, stigmatized heroes find themselves in a supremely multivalent condition, since their physiognomy publicly proclaims them as in some sense morally transcendent, mediators both necessary and dangerous.

The climactic events of the mythic cycle of Jesus fit exactly this model of stigma as an element of sacrifice. First, Jesus is equated at a Passover feast with a sacrificial lamb, a confusion of boundaries perpetuated and intensified by the disciples' symbolic feasting upon his flesh and blood. This image is completed on the Friday of Passover, when Jesus is suspended on the cross to die both as a physical and a spiritual mediator between earth and heaven, just as if he were a Mosaic sacrifice. Significantly, the instant of Jesus' death is punctuated by the tearing in two of the Temple curtain that separates the human from the divine (Leach 1976: 87). These events are the common fund of the synoptic gospels.

Second, we have already observed that the stigmata which Jesus bears as a result of his crucifixion are indications simultaneously of physical mortality and of spiritual immortality.

Third, the transcendent morality which Jesus represents is emphasized in the gospels by the messianic aspects of his career: for example, the disciples' refusal (with Jesus' approval) to wash their hands; Jesus' association with tax-collectors and prostitutes; attacks upon the property structure of Hebrew society and upon its generational and ecclestiastical authority structure; Jesus' denial of basic kinship ties; and Jesus' claims of prophetic status.

The case of Cain is rather more difficult to interpret, since modern audiences usually draw from this myth only a moral injunction against murder. However, the fourth chapter of Genesis may be interpreted as representing the murder of Abel by Cain as a direct solution to the inferiority of Cain's non-sanguinary offerings (this interpretation is consistent with the implications of the chart in Leach 1967: 7): there is a fine irony implied when God has rejected as sacrifice the pious offerings of Cain the farmer, expressing a preference for the products of Abel the herder, only to be offered as an alternative sacrifice the herder himself! If we take into account the standard literary and mythological device of characterizing twins or siblings as a means of displaying opposed qualities of a single hero (a theme analyzed by Rank, Radin, Bettelheim, Dumézil, and Lévi-Strauss, to name only a few), then we immediately perceive that Cain has sacrificed the 'animal'-related aspect of himself. I have already pointed out that the stigmatization consequent upon the murder carries with it the contradictory implications of physical mortality and spiritual or social immortality, and that Cain's immunity from vengeance is hardly consistent with Old-Testament moral standards.

4. Stigma and the theme of the trickster

We may identify the mythic hero who stands at the nexus of mortality and immortality, structure and antistructure, the individual and society, as a *trickster*, found in mythologies throughout the world (Radin 1972; note also the fairly comprehensive list given by Edmonson 1971: 142). A trickster, as the term itself suggests, plays tricks upon the beings – humans, gods, and animals – who people the mythologic universe, with the overt intention of making the victims look foolish despite their professed wisdom or strength (the trickster is often a creature of characteristic weakness or timidity, such as a mouse or rabbit). These pranks are frequently a combination of the violent and the scatological (both, I presume, intimating mortality), and in some cultural traditions rebound upon the trickster, who thereby befools himself. On one level of interpretation, it is clear that the trickster is Everyman caught in an existential dilemma of Sartrean proportions, and that the somewhat morbid humour which results must be understood from a perspective which would not be unfamiliar to a Zen adept. On another level of interpretation, it is relevant to note that the corpus of trickster-tales nearly always includes an origin myth which offers an explanation for human mortality on the one hand, and for various facets of social art or craft on the other. Thus the 'trick' played is to transcend ordinary reality by violating it in such a way (through obscenity and violence) that society is simultaneously disrupted and renewed – an act of creation with death as its inescapable attendant.

These levels of interpretation are drawn together by the fate of the trickster, who is to be physically damaged or demarcated (never killed) by the very trick that produces both death and creativity: Prometheus must bear the vulture that devours his entrails (which are daily renewed), just as tricksters of North and South America are often impaled by a sharp stick in the anus (a wound which is understandably annoying, but apparently rarely fatal). In other words, the stigmatization of the trickster *is* the sacrifice he makes to gift human society with death and creativity. Would it be too far-fetched to include the stigmata of Cain and Jesus in this genre? When all is said and done, I cannot but imagine that the early Hebrews may have enjoyed the discomfiture of the somewhat stodgy and irascible Yahweh upon learning of the ironic sacrifice that Cain had made him, every bit as much as the early Christians may have rejoiced when Jesus outsmarted the excessively formalistic Sadducees and Pharisees in verbal exchange.

Conclusion

My conclusions have clearly preceded me above, so I shall merely observe that my analysis of Jesus and Cain by no means exhausts the range of stigmatized Biblical heroes; the example of Jacob/Israel springs to mind, as does the Whore of Babylon (Rev. 17.5).

Notes

1 I would like to thank Dr Norman Buchignani, Sir Edmund Leach, Dr Keith Parry, and Dr Brent Shaw for reading and criticizing various earlier versions of this essay.

2 Professor I. Schapera (1955) has previously discussed the mark of Cain in an anthropological context, but with a very different purpose – to cast light on

Old Testament legal norms. I perceive his essay and mine as directed towards ends which may be regarded as complementary, not mutually exclusive.

3 All references in this paper are to the Revised Standard Edition of the Christian Bible.

4 I am indebted to Sir Edmund Leach for the acute observation that a stigma ought to be regarded, among other things, as a mark of ownership by a deity.

5 Leviticus, of course, prescribes that both a sacrificial animal and a priest are initially consecrated by virtue of being *without* blemish. I take it that this later heightens the contrast when during the ritual of sacrifice both animal and priest are stigmatized by the blood of the former.

References

Becker, Ernest 1973 *The Denial of Death*, New York: Free Press

Cohen, Percy 1969 'Theories of Myth', in *Man* (n.s.) 4: 337–53.

Douglas, Mary 1966 *Purity and Danger; an Analysis of Concepts of Pollution and Taboo*, London: Routledge and Kegan Paul

Edmonson, M. S. 1971 *Lore; an Introduction to the Science of Folklore and Literature*, New York: Holt, Rinehart, and Winston

Geertz, Clifford 1966 'Religion as a cultural system', in M. Banton (ed.) *Anthropological Approaches to the Study of Religion*, A.S.A. Monographs 3, London: Tavistock

Goffman, Erving 1963 *Stigma; Notes on the Management of Spoiled Identity*, Englewood Cliffs, N.J.: Prentice-Hall

Hubert, Henri and Mauss, Marcel 1964 *Sacrifice: its Nature and Function*, Chicago: University of Chicago Press

Leach, Edmund 1967 *Genesis as Myth and Other Essays*
    1976 *Culture and Communication: the Logic by which Symbols are Connected*, Cambridge: Cambridge University Press.

Radin, Paul 1972 *The Trickster; a Study in American Indian Mythology*, New York: Schocken Books

Schapera, Isaac 1955 'The Sin of Cain', in *Journal of the Royal Anthropological Institute of Great Britain and Northern Ireland* 85: 33–43

Soler, Paul 1979 'The Dietary Prohibitions of the Hebrews', in *New York Review of Books* 26(10): 24–30

Turner, Victor 1967 'Symbols in Ndembu Ritual', in *The Forest of Symbols*, Ithaca, N.Y.: Cornell University Press
    1969 *The Ritual Process; Structure and Anti-structure*, London: Routledge and Kegan Paul
    1970 'Introduction', in *Forms of Symbolic Action*, R. F. Spencer (ed.), Proceedings of the 1969 Annual Spring Meeting of the American Ethnological Society, Seattle: University of Washington Press
    1974 'Social Dramas and Ritual Metaphors', in *Dramas, Fields, and Metaphors; Symbolic Action in Human Society*, Ithaca, N.Y.: Cornell University Press
    1977 'Sacrifice as quintessential process: prophylaxis or abandonment?', *History of Religions* 16: 189–215

Tylor, E. B. 1958 (First ed. 1871) *Primitive Culture*, 2 vols., New York: Harper and Brothers
Veblen, Thorstein 1953 *The Theory of the Leisure Class*, Toronto: New American Library

Author Index

Index of biblical references

130

131

Biblical references